RETIRED COP'S GUIDE TO SCHOOL SURVIVAL

RETIRED COP'S GUIDE TO SCHOOL SURVIVAL

FROM HANDCUFFS TO HALL PASSES: NAVIGATING HIGH SCHOOL MADNESS

JOSH UHERNIK

CONTENTS

INTRODUCTION

As Chris Farely said in the movie "Tommy Boy" HOLY SCHNIKES!" I never thought I'd be writing a book about law enforcement and education and how it's tied together! But here I am about to share the secrets of the high school classroom (not really), but I may know a thing or two about teaching. So, let's jump into what this book is about and hopefully there is something you find valuable enough to take to your own classroom. Oh, and if anything else, just enjoy the banter of those high school brains and hormones.

People always ask me why I left education for a career in law enforcement (and no it wasn't for the coffee and doughnuts). They comment on how much different the two careers must be. My response is that education and teaching are not that much different than law enforcement. In fact, I tell them that being a teacher prepared me for a life of patrolling the streets. Now law enforcement has prepared me for a life of patrolling the hallways (minus the handcuffs and pepper spray). I then go on to explain that education has taught me organizational skills, report writing, conflict resolution, communication skills, and many other important lessons of life needed to be a police officer. I completely give credit to what was then, my seven years of being in education, for preparing me to be successful in my law enforcement career.

Fast forwarding sixteen years, here I am being asked the opposite question. The question now is what made me switch from law enforcement back into teaching. I always answer this question the same way in that teaching has always been my calling. Even while in law enforcement I was a teacher. I trained new officers, taught at the police academy, and held trainings for departments around my area. I am also currently traveling the country presenting at seminars and conferences educating officers and school officials around the world. A lot of the perspectives and strategies I had implemented before, came from the courses I took in college. I didn't have a lot of life experience to add to my teaching style. Now with 16 years of police work, I have those life skills and experiences to apply to the classroom. I can teach my students deeper and more meaningful real-life skills that I didn't know how to teach before. That's the goal of this book. I want to share my journey from teaching to law enforcement and then back to teaching. I am by no means an expert in education. Some of my teaching strategies are not by the book. But at the end of the day, my students will be prepared for the real world and graduate. So grab hold of that coffee and that box of unsharpened pencils because we are about take a voyage into the classroom of a former police officer who is trying to survive the world of high school.......

HOLY SCHNIKES!!

PART ONE
FROM CUFFS TO CLASSROOMS

MY TRANSITION FROM THE BADGE TO THE DESK

When I decided to write a book, the first thing that crossed my mind was, "Who is going to want to read a book about a police officer who transitioned back into teaching". Not only did I question who my audience would be, but why would they read it? Then I realized that anyone who goes from another career to teaching has life experiences that they pull from to help them adapt to a new job. I thought if I could share my own experiences and how I applied those strategies from law enforcement, it may help guide someone else who is on the path to the classroom. I'm not saying that everything I do in the classroom would work for everyone who reads this book, but it's a place to start when you may have some doubts about teaching or need to find the humor in being a teacher. So here we go! Welcome to Jurassic Park! Now put that coffee down and grab something a little bit stronger (You're going to need an alcoholic beverage for this). I promise no field sobriety tests or breathalyzers. Just dive in and get ready for a rollercoaster ride called High School.

Here it is. The great transition from the badge to the desk, or as I like to call it, "From Handcuffs to Hall Passes." You might imagine that going from being a police officer to a special education teacher is akin to switching from a high-speed chase to a slow stroll in the park but let me assure you-it's the kind of park where the slide is broken, and there are squirrels conspiring against you. I remember my first day in the classroom vividly. The décor screamed, "Welcome to the shit show" and I felt like a newly minted rookie stepping into the wild world of high school for the first time. It was all a bit surreal. One moment, I was donning my badge, navigating the city's streets, and munching on a donut, and the next, I was armed with nothing more than a dry-erase marker and a Chromebook that I wasn't given a password for.

As a cop, my day was dictated by a strict schedule -patrolling the streets, responding to emergencies, and, oh yes, throw in a few barking dogs! In contrast, the teaching world felt like stepping into a circus, albeit one where the students who were getting all worked up over the latest "tea" which means "rumors" in a teenager's vocabulary. I found that I was so out of touch with the teenage culture, that I realized I needed to catch up quick or it would be a hell of a year.

My very first day, I sat in the classroom that I later would be confined to for an entire year. There were no windows, no air circulating -imagine the smell of a warm turtle tank, and no way out!

I was introduced to the special education department and the peers I would be working with. With the addition of me to the department, we had one hell of a dynamic educator group.

We were like the island of misfit toys where administration threw us food on a regular basis just to keep the hangry side of us at bay. The first team member I met was our department head. Imagine a guy who may have had a tiny stature, but he meant business. He was organized, creative, and the students loved him. This gentleman was our rock. I learned so much from this man that when he decide to move on from the in-person education, it made me think all was lost. I felt like my crutch was taken away and now I'd have to rely on my next teammate.

Enter teammate number two. At first glance I was impressed by her demeanor and personality. She stood before me as a bilingual teacher who looked as if she could conquer anything. As the weeks went on, I saw a little rowdiness in her. She was a short, proud Hispanic woman to carried herself incredibly well. Now as I got to know her better, it became apparent that her spirit animal was surely a Chihuahua. The "Chihuahua" as she soon was now known as, would bite your head off if you even looked at her wrong. I did find the secret to calming the beast inside her though and it was a box of nutty buddy's! It reminded me of the Snickers commercials where a man turns into a drama queen and then BAM! He eats a Snickers and he's back to being calm. Throw one at her from across the room and all was fine.

This group was our mild/mod class. I can't forget our significant needs and Transition staff. This group of ladies had it rough. They had so many different students with different needs. It was like walking into Dunkin Donuts and seeing all the flavors and varieties. Each student was unique and awesome! The loss of teachers and paraprofessionals throughout the school made that class difficult. However, every day they continue to show up and care for those kids through thick and thin. They all are an inspiration because they look those difficulties in the eye and say, "not today!"

Moving back to the classroom on my first day, it was a reading remediation class. I stared at 12 freshman whose eyes were all on me. The comments of "who is that?" and "why is this dude in our class?" filled the air as curiosity struck. Everyone was on edge wanting to know who I was. I didn't let the class know that a few of them looked like some juveniles I had arrested in the past (didn't want to get off on the wrong foot).

For four months I worked on building relationships and earning the students' trust. By the end of that fourth month, I had a group of 12 students who would end up being more loyal to me than any police officer I ever worked with. As far as a happy ending goes, well it wasn't that simple. That trust weathered a lot of good days and bad days. Behavior was the first obstacle I needed to address. Going from half the class speaking Spanish and not knowing what the hell they were talking about, to testing my patience seeing how far they could go with that 3-inch rope. So, I asked myself, what behavior strategies could I implement to get the class back on track? One classroom management strategy I inherited from my law enforcement days was the ability to maintain a confident, authoritative stance on my expectations.

However, my "don't mess with me" look seemed to send my students into fits of fear rather than compliance. There I was, trying to channel my inner Serpico, while my students were busy rating my potential as a possible serial killer. Trust me; it's a humbling experience when you're trying to gain respect but end up having a group of students look at you as the main character of Stephen King novel. I may have been that intimidating force in the classroom, but little did they know, I had a sense of humor too. When a few pushed my buttons to see how far they could go, I had to remind them that I've dealt with tougher crowds, like the suspects in an interrogation room.

But somehow, trying to intimidate a room full of immature teens felt like a lost cause. In leadership they say that you don't want your team to fear you, you want them to fear to disappoint you. In this case, I didn't want my students to fear me. This is not the road that was going to get them to the finish line. My goal was to give them the confidence and determination to get to that finish line because that was their goal. I committed to seeing them there no matter the circumstances.

In those early months, I quickly learned that teenagers have unique and often baffling behaviors. Instead of addressing delinquency, I found myself managing cell phone usage, hats, and explaining why it's not appropriate to reenact scenes from "Die Hard" during algebra. Let's not forget navigating the treacherous waters of lunchroom drama and who's going to win the next arm-wrestling match. Gone were the days of asking for ID on a traffic stop; it was now, "Can you please stop tossing that pizza across the room?"

When I finally got the hang of things, I realized that my background equipped me with quite a few skills that could come in handy. Conflict resolution, for example, became a natural fit for me in the classroom. Instead of working to defuse a married couple arguing, I was mediating disputes involving pencil theft and who took the last glue stick from the closet. Let me tell you, those battles can be just as fierce! "No, Kim, you can't have a snack right now; at least wait until I finish my coffee!" Eventually, I learned that just as in law enforcement, the key is to be calm under pressure. I assure you, it's just as important to keep your cool when you're facing a student who insists they've "definitely done the homework" but can't seem to produce the evidence.

What I didn't anticipate was how similar the fundamental forces of human behavior would be in both law enforcement and education. In both fields, I found myself trying to understand people's motivations, whether they were students vying for an A or suspects caught in a clip from "Cops." My experiences on the force made me less likely to take things personally. After all, if Icould handle a suspect yelling at me about his innocent, pet goldfish, I could definitely manage a few rolling eyes from a high schooler. "You think you've got it bad?" I wanted to shout. "I've seen real chaos in the real world! Try leading a pursuit of a stolen handicapped chair! It will change your perspective!

In all seriousness, the transition from the badge to the desk has had a few ups and downs, just like any good comedy. There were days I threw my hands up and thought, "What in the world have I gotten myself into?" But ultimately, I discovered something deeper and far more fulfilling than mere discipline and order. I found passion, purpose, and a life-changing opportunity to help young minds shape their futures. I knew that while it may take some getting used to, the truth is, being a retired cop in a classroom isn't just a punchline; it's a chance to impact lives with humor, heart, and a little bit of discipline on the side. After all what better way to educate than with a bit of laughter?

UNDERSTANDING HIGH SCHOOL CULTURE

High school culture.... If I had a nickel for every time I thought I understood it, I'd still have just a nickel - a shiny reminder of my naiveté. I came into the world of law enforcement thinking that having a badge would give me some magical insight into the social dynamics of teenagers. Instead, I was immediately thrust into the intricacies of a world where social hierarchies mind-boggled even the world's most well-intentioned superheroes. I quickly learned that if you want to survive in high school, picking up on the subtleties of the culture is as crucial as remembering to count the number of students sneaking off to the bathroom to vape during your lecture.

It's a realm filled with eye rolls, whispered secrets, and an inordinate amount of texting, even in the classroom. This is a phenomenon much like Skin Walker Ranch that I don't believe even the CIA could infiltrate. Teenagers possess a sixth sense of communication that involves emojis, abbreviations, and, on occasion, actual words (but only if absolutely necessary). My policing background didn't prepare me for this. Attempting to decipher teenage slang can often feel like chasing a suspect through a maze while blindfolded. "What's the 4n on your homework?" feels triumphant until you discover that you've inadvertently asked if anyone knows how to order pizza instead. Note to self: Context clues matter, especially when it relates to sustenance.

High school culture operates on its own set of laws, a subculture that is both fascinating and frustrating. The hierarchy is especially intriguing - let me tell you, the popular kids can strut around like they're auditioning for a role in "America's Next Top Model." Watching them gel their hair for an hour only for it to be deemed "so last week" can be jaw-dropping. But, folks, those undercurrents run deep! One moment, I'm explaining Shakespeare, and the next, I'm embroiled in a heated debate about which TikTok dance is the best. I mean, my expertise is in law enforcement, not as a judge from "America's Got Talent".

As a retired cop-turned-teacher, my initial mission was straightforward: impart knowledge and keep order. What I didn't realize was how wonderfully chaotic high school would be. Enter the "dramatic declarations" phase - yes, you know what I mean. In one swift motion, the popular girl might announce, "I'm done with Jamie!" I'm cutting her off" while simultaneously filming a TikTok reenacting the tragic event. Meanwhile, Jamie will block her on Instagram from across the room, replete with exaggerated expressions worthy of an Oscar. It's a soap opera that plays out every day, right in front of me. All I can do is nod and wonder if I could get away with a dramatic monologue about my time on the force.

Now, let's talk about the cafeteria because, my friends, it's a breeding ground for all things dramatic, delicious, and downright bizarre. This is the arena where the unwritten rules come alive! Picture it: a chorus of lunch trays clattering, the waft of questionable meatloaf, and social dynamics as complex as a Shakespearean tragedy. There are the "Cool Kids' Tables", the "Jocks", the "band kids", and the "loaners." Each one of these groups engaged in their own dialogue and actions. I quickly established a non-existent social contract, navigating which tables were off-limits for faculty and where I could sit without accidentally starting an international incident. Trust me, if you want to eat your salad in peace, you better tread carefully!

Navigating high school culture as a teacher requires a careful balance of authority and approachability, much like walking a tightrope while juggling flaming torches. The sweet spot lies somewhere between being the "cool teacher" and the "don't mess with me" teacher. You want them to respect you but also feel comfortable enough to come to you with their emergencies (like that sudden "I forgot to do my homework" panic that inevitably strikes every Thursday). Slowly but surely, I began to build connections with students, and soon I realized that once they felt safe, they actually let me into their world.

In the end, understanding high school culture means embracing the chaos and turmoil, and navigating the social waters with the grace of a hippo on a trampoline. I may not have all the answers, but I assure you that my experiences taught me that laughter and connection go a long way - both with students and fellow teachers. And so, as I step into tomorrow's classroom, I'm armed not just with lesson plans, but with a newfound conviction to embrace this wild ride. Who knew that teaching would feel more like directing my own sitcom? With glitter, drama, and a splash of teenage chaos at every turn, lucky for me, I've got the badge to prove I can handle just about anything - well, except maybe the lunchroom mystery meat.

COMMON MISCONCEPTIONS ABOUT TEACHERS

Everyone has heard, "Oh you're a teacher? Must be nice to have summers off, snow days, and holiday vacations". Although those statements are true, the noble profession of teaching is a realm often clouded by misconceptions thicker than a teenager's excuse for why he was gone oto the bathroom for half the class. You know, the old adage that goes, "Those who can, do; those who can't, teach?" Yeah, I could write an entire chapter debunking that one alone, while simultaneously doing a headstand on the front desk! The world seems to have conjured a myriad of beliefs about us teachers that could only come from someone who believes they're in the next blockbuster romantic comedy. Let's pull back the curtain and shine a light on these assumptions, shall we? Buckle up; it's about to get a little bumpy!

First off, let's address the notion that teachers have an infinite supply of free time. Ha! This idea was so entrenched in my mind that I thought my buddies from the force would spend their weekends relaxing at a tropical resort while I was grading papers in a caffeine-fueled stupor. Spoiler alert: I was the one working late in a dimly lit classroom, praying for the sweet release of the final bell while simultaneously Googling "I love grading papers." You'll laugh, but I'd actually be lying if I didn't admit to Googling "How to Survive Infinite Paperwork" as if it were a self-help book.

Many people seem to think that teachers live this enviable life of endless summer vacations and holiday breaks that resemble a scene straight out of a Coca-Cola commercial. The truth? Sure, we do enjoy some time off, but when those vacation weeks arrive, we're often stacked high with lesson plans, curriculum development, and oh yeah, reflecting on whether to reintroduce the electric slide during the upcoming school dance. I'll tell you, the irony of being on a beach while your mind races over how to turn "a motor vehicle accident" into a physics lesson on the Pythagorean Theorem gives a whole new meaning to "working remotely."

Next on the list of unfounded opinions is the myth that all teachers are superhumans who can always maintain perfect composure. Let's get real for a moment here. If I had a dollar for every time I've found myself staring blankly at a student who just said, "I didn't know we had a quiz," I could retire and finally escape this circus for a sun-kissed hammock in Destin Florida! Despite popular belief, I'm not a statue or an impenetrable force. There are days when my patience is stretched thinner than a high school hallway rumor, and students take the brunt of my slip-ups! My inside voice may yell, "Not again!" while my outside voice takes a deep breath and calmly explains why "the dog ate it" doesn't quite cut it as an excuse.

Another amusing, yet cringe-worthy misconception is that teachers have eyes in the back of their heads. Sure, I've honed my observational skills over a decade of policing, but I've yet to sprout an extra appendage on my head that grants me a panoramic view of the classroom. On particularly chaotic days, I feel like a referee in a wrestling match, dodging flying objects, multipurpose pens, and the occasional glances of students who are way too proud of their latest TikTok moves. In those moments, I can assure you no amount of "teacher intuition" will save you from being pelted with that rubber chicken from across the room.

Now, let's not forget the belief that teachers live by some sort of mystical code of wisdom and know everything about the subjects they teach. Think of us as feisty lifelong learners, navigating our subjects like a kid trying to navigate the mall for the first time. Every day is a discovery and trust me when I say, don't always trust your students to teach you how to speak "appropriate Spanish" That's right, folks! Teachers learn on the fly, and you may be surprised to know that my communication skills with the Hispanic students have gotten better, but what my students have taught me, can't be published in this book.

Underneath all the misconceptions lies a simple truth: we teachers are just trying to make sense of the swirling waters known as high school culture while simultaneously imparting wisdom and inspiration. Contrary to popular belief, we're not superheroes; we're just ordinary humans navigating extraordinary challenges, fueled by caffeinated brews and a determination to make a difference one sarcastic remark at a time.

So, the next time you encounter a teacher, remember that

we're often juggling the perception of being all-knowing, tire-less, and perpetually on vacation, all the while trying to foster a productive environment where kids can thrive. If you hear voices echoing the universal truth that we're all in this together, it's probably coming from the lunch table where we exchange war stories - just like retired cops after a long tour of duty!

FINDING YOUR TEACHING STYLE

Finding your teaching style is like trying to locate a unicorn at a theme park: it feels utterly magical, yet almost entirely elusive. When I first stepped into the classroom, I was confronted by a joyful mix of expectations, uncertainty, and let's be honest, an overwhelming fear of being compared to the last "poor soul" whose spot I took. Much like walking into a high-stakes negotiation meeting, I quickly realized that understanding how to connect with high schoolers was less about having a polished approach and more about rolling with the punches while simultaneously deciphering which students are genuinely interested versus those who would rather be watching cat videos on their phones.

Imagine my surprise when I discovered that my early attempts at finding my teaching style resulted in more comedic missteps than educational clarity. Picture it: my grandiose plan for a riveting lesson on the impact of the fourth amendment in law enforcement suddenly collapsed when a student raised his hand to passionately debate inequality in the Roblox video game loot boxes instead. I quickly learned that the principles of "teaching" I brought from the force, needed to be adjusted significantly. If I didn't do this, I'd end up exchanging riveting tales of misdemeanors while intermingling it with lessons on "how to score bonus points in Fortnite."

After a few cringe-worthy lessons (don't even ask about my attempt to use law enforcement analogies), I found the key was to embrace authenticity. I realized I didn't have to wear an invisible cape or try to emulate every famed educator I admired from afar. Instead, I decided to stick with my unique blend of humor, storytelling, and the occasional quip about how my life used to revolve around chasing suspects instead of chasing down the definition of 'photosynthesis.' Never underestimate the ability of a well-timed joke about arresting a poorly drawn superhero to connect with your students. Laughter is a universal language—especially when it comes to conveying that I'm more than just a guy who handed out citations in the real world.

In the search for my teaching style, I stumbled into experimentation. Yes, you guessed it, my classroom quickly became a mad scientist's laboratory! I tried incorporating everything from juggling apples while explaining how to use context clues when answering reading comprehension questions, to innovative group projects that ended with students recreating famous historical events with dance routines. While creativity limited my ability to mold perfect lessons, it opened a door to student engagement that turned class discussions into raucous brainstorming sessions worthy of a comedy club.

There's something infectious about a scenario where students feel comfortable enough to express their ideas. Trust me; it's not the result of some elaborate scheme but rather the power of unfiltered conversation. Teaching, I realized, isn't just about sheer knowledge; it's about weaving students' voices into the fabric of the classroom. My style evolved into being a facilitator of conversations-encouraging them to share their perspectives while simultaneously quizzing them about how this might coincide with persuading someone to leave their gaming console for a mere hour of studying (I've yet to crack that mystery).

Naturally, we all know that the high school experience is rife with the socially awkward and sometimes absurd. Learning to embrace my own quirks, therefore, became just as important as guiding my students through history and science truths. Regaling tales from my years as a cop, I would invoke connections between the principles of law enforcement and the precarity of an algebraic equation. "Consider it a chase-the suspects are the variables, and your goal is to catch them!" Just try to resist a snicker when you find a student excited about solving equations-a victory lap born from the thrill of mastering the art of mathematics!

By opening my classroom doors as both a teacher and a fellow flawed human, I discovered that vulnerability is equally powerful as authority. Students began to see me as someone relatable and imperfect rather than an omniscient being on a pedestal. My teaching style morphed into a delightful patchwork; I showcased my authenticity wrapped in laughter while guiding their hearts and minds into new territories of understanding.

Eventually, I learned that part of finding your teaching style involves weaving your life's experiences into the very fabric of your approach. Whether that includes humor, targeted storytelling, or an inexplicable ability to reference "Law and Order" episodes in a historical context, no two teachers are the same. I quickly realized that this is precisely what makes teaching such an exciting and rewarding profession. Well, that and the constant surprise of which student will redefine your day with a random question about the scariest time I had as a police officer. So much like a seasoned investigator closing a case, I can proudly declare: that my teaching style has emerged as the one that celebrates both the chaos and the joy of learning - one hilariously unpredictable lesson at a time!

THE SURPRISING SIMILARITIES BETWEEN COPS AND EDUCATORS

You might think that the worlds of law enforcement and education are separated by a chasm so deep that not even a well-thrown rubber chicken can bridge it. Once I swapped my badge for a dry-erase marker, I found myself pleasantly surprised by the similarities. In fact, as I've spent time navigating the unpredictable waters of high school life, I've come toappreciate the uncanny parallels that exist between being a cop and being an educator. Grab some popcorn while I break down the most amusing (and occasionally ridiculous) revelations I've had along this journey.

First off, let's talk about managing chaos. Whether it's a classroom of high schoolers playing "Dodge the Teacher" with their cell phones, or a ruckus on the streets involving mischief-makers, chaos is a constant companion in both professions. Picture it: you're standing in front of your class, explaining the finer points of Shakespeare, when suddenly, a feminine napkin swoops by, narrowly missing your head. In that moment, you realize that managing chaos isn't just about imposing control; it's about adapting to the madness in such a way that keeps everybody engaged and entertained.

Both cops and educators also sport finely tuned observational skills. Just like a cop on patrol, you quickly learn to read the demeanor of those around you. Everywhere I go I am observing. If I go to a nice Olive Garden dinner, I'm scanning the restaurant for past arrestees and escape routes. It's not just something you can turn off, so you have to embrace it. In the classroom it's no different. If you observe Billy has mysteriously transformed from an enthusiastic scholar to a brooding lump on the desk, you can bet something's up. Maybe he's met with the same fate as the last of my precious donut stash! The ability to pick up on subtle cues - be it a nervous tap of a pencil or the way a student has completely written off their homework-can mean the difference between turning a small issue into a teachable moment or letting it spiral into an all-out revolt. You don't need a crystal ball to make observations, just a closely honed instinct for sensing underlying tension.

Let's not forget the importance of communication. Law enforcement relies heavily on effective dialogue to diffuse a situation - just as educators must navigate the foggy maze of teenage interaction. You'd be astounded by the variety of ways to express yourself in both worlds: barking orders to calm a crowd or teaching methods to pacify potential teenage drama. You find ways to ensure your message is clear-whether it's emphasizing the need for being quiet during tests or reminding students (for the hundreth time) that "the restroom passes are not for playing tag in the hallway." Both careers require you to be quick on your feet, armed with words sharper than a marijuana grinder in a repeat offender's backpack.

Then you have the element of empathy. Sure, you may not think a tough cop who's dealt with a real crime would share anything with a soft-hearted teacher who still believes in the magic of color-coded sticky notes. But both roles stem from a place of caring. The ability to put yourself in another's shoes is critical whether you're talking a teenager down from a ledge of drama or dealing with an irate citizen who believes they've been wrongly accused by the HOA of not stuffing their trash fully into the bin. It's about understanding the underlying emotions then stripping away that bravado. Now you may just uncover a hurting human who desperately needs support, guidance, and maybe a slice of pizza.

As an educator, you often find yourself serving as a community resource-a guiding hand that connects students with their peers, mentors, and sometimes even their parents (which, let's face it, can also look like an interrogation room). The best cops do the same, engaging with their neighborhoods, promoting safety, and building relationships that make everyone feel valued. It's all about establishing trust and making sure people realize you're there not as a judge but as an advocate. I've found that whether I'm trying to connect with a hesitant student or de-escalate an issue in the hallways, a friendly smile often works better than any disciplinary piece of paper. The saying is true, "You catch more flies with honey than you do vinegar."

Finally, I've come to appreciate the mounds of paperwork that ensue in both professions. Yes, my friends, this is a surefire way to bond!! Just like filing police reports after a long day, educators tackle mountains of assignments and checks for understanding. Don't even get me started on IEPs! You can almost hear the groans from administrators and teachers alike as we dive into paperwork, fretting over grammar errors while being propelled by midnight coffee and desperate stamina. The amount of paperwork that you do can be very intimidating. On top of just the amount, you then have to validate, finalize and face a possible audit. If timelines aren't met, if accommodations are not given, and if the correct boxes aren't checked, here comes the lawsuits. It is almost a rite of passage, trial by fire!

So, there you have it the surprising similarities between cops and educators manifest through the absurdities, challenges, and rewards of our everyday lives. Navigating chaos, building rapport, and nurturing the community bonds we share, all remind us that, at our core, we're in this together. We are in it to uplift, guide, and occasionally deliver a good punchline to make things lighter. I've learned that whether you're policing the streets or teaching in a classroom, you might just find yourself laughing amid the chaos as you try to figure out which teacher is responsible for the fart box hidden under your desk. After all, in both jobs, laughter trumps everything, and it turns out we could all use a few more chuckles along the way!

PART TWO
UNDERSTANDING TEEN BEHAVIOR

THE EVOLVING TEEN BRAIN

The teen brain - the most mysterious and puzzling biological entity known to humankind. If you've ever tried to decipher the strange behaviors of a teenager, you know exactly what I'm talking about. It's like trying to solve a Rubik's Cube blindfolded while riding a unicycle. One moment they're laughing and carefree ready to conquer the world, and the next, they're melting down over a B+ like their entire life's aspirations just crumbled into dust. What gives? Enter the evolving teen brain, stage left, complete with a dramatic flair worthy of any high school drama club.

First off, let's talk about the wiring that's going on inside their noggins. The teenage brain is undergoing a transformation that gives it the energy of a hyperactive squirrel on espresso. While the prefrontal cortex - the place where logic, decision-making, and impulse control nestles - takes its sweet time developing, the amygdala, the emotion center of the brain, is fully operational and firing on all cylinders. This is practically the emotional equivalent of handing a toddler a paintbrush and asking them to create a masterpiece, all while a massive storm rolls in. Yes, you'll see bursts of creativity and passion, but there's also a lot of messiness, tantrums, and maybe a few flying paintbrushes. The end result is a beautifully chaotic mind that often leads to confused parents and educators like myself trying to figure out whether they should offer wisdom or simply step aside and let the storm pass.

Perhaps the most charming aspect of this developmental circus is the cognitive dissonance at play. One moment, teens believe they have the world figured out. They're the next Greta Thunberg or Elon Musk, armed with opinions sharper than their newly acquired driver's licenses. Then, in a blink, they're knee-deep in existential crises, wondering why their crush hasn't texted back in 20 min. Did they accidentally send a meme instead of a heart emoji? The anxiety is real! It's an internal battle reminiscent of cops dealing with a runaway suspect: a lot of noise and confusion but very little rational thought.

So, as an educator, I find myself navigating these emotional roller coasters daily. I like to think of my students as members of a high-stakes game show where the prize is sheer survival. There's the "Who Wants to Be Emotionally Fit?" segment, where I'm trying to help them process their erratic feelings without losing all their marbles. "Congratulations! You've successfully refrained from an emotional breakdown today - now onto the next round!" The stakes are high, especially when you realize that the fate of their futures, and maybe just a little bit of your sanity, rides on every quiz score and social media post.

And forget about multitasking! Have you ever watched a teenager attempt to do homework while scrolling through TikTok and simultaneously responding to their friends' group chat? It's like witnessing a three-ring circus where the trapeze artists are juggling flaming swords, and the tightrope walkers are wearing roller skates. News flash: their attention span is shorter than the span of your average TikTok video. As a teacher, I pick my battles wisely. If a note gets passed in class-likely detailing who said what about whom in the cafeteria-I'm more inclined to see how I can turn that into a teachable moment rather than unleash my inner police officer and confiscate it.

And let's not overlook the ever-changing social landscape that is high school life. Teens are not just trying to figure out their identity; they're also battling the societal expectations tossed their way like confetti at a parade. The quest for popularity? A deadly combination of fierce competition, unfiltered opinions, and unwritten rules that can flip on a dime. It's like watching a group of hawks circling around a single piece of pizza. One minute they're chirping their admiration for each other, and the next, they're engaged in a savage feud over who wore it better at prom.

So, there you have it, the evolving teenage brain in all its alien-like splendor! It's a wild ride filled with creativity, confusion, and the occasional outburst over how someone took the last slice of pizza. As an educator, I've learned that patience is key, and humor is a powerful weapon in this never-ending battle of wills. My goal? To guide these wonderfully chaotic minds through the labyrinth of teenage angst, one laugh and lesson at a time. And if all else fails, I keep a stash of nutty buttys in my desk because nothing bridges the communication gap quite like snacks.

SOCIAL DYNAMICS AMONG TEENS

The social dynamics among teens - a chaotic world that rivals even the most dramatic reality TV shows. It's packed with plot twists, secret alliances, and let's not forget, an overabundance of snack drama. If you've ever had the pleasure of watching a group of teenagers interact, you'll know it's like witnessing a live performance of Shakespeare's "The Tempest", only with more eye-rolling, fewer epic speeches, and an unending supply of avocados. Yes, avocados! Because, you see, the teen social scene is as nuanced as a perfectly ripe slice of avocado toast-complex, occasionally messy, and highly susceptible to trends.

At the apex of this social hierarchy, you have the "popular kids." They tread the hallways with an air of confidence that can only be described as "I woke up like this" meets "How did I just become the prom queen?"

They hold the power of social currency, and their acceptance or rejection can make or break one's self-esteem faster than a

TikTok dance trend. In their world, liking the wrong meme or wearing last season's shoes can lead to an emotional nosedive stronger than an intoxicated driver who's 3 times the legal limit doing the one legged stand. It's a cutthroat ecosystem where everyone is vying for a spot at the top, and every friendship comes with an expiration date.

Then you have the "artsy kids," the ones who walk around with oversized sweaters and a deep emotional connection to their sketchbooks. They might seem eccentric, but insiders know they're the true trendsetters. One day they'll be singing their praises for obscure bands you've never heard of, and the next, they'll be creating a viral art project that spirals way out of control. It's a delicate balancing act between expressing themselves and trying not to become the subject of the next social media roast. Honestly, I admire their bravery; they're like the platypus of the social ecosystem, totally unique and not afraid to be themselves, all the while keeping a watchful eye on the latest mood ring colors.

The "sports kids", on the other hand, are living in their own universe. They strut around in jerseys, carrying the weight of high expectations on their shoulders. Social events? They'd rather be on the field. Practices and games are sacred, and don't you dare challenge their dedication, or you'll face the wrath of a group of adrenaline-fueled15-year-olds. Watching a jock try to navigate the social challenges of high school is like watching a lion on a treadmill: they move with undeniable power, but put them too close to the plunge, and that approach can lead to inevitable disaster.

In the midst of all these factions, there are the "floater kids." You know, the ones with the elusive butterfly quality, flitting from group to group like it's an Olympic sport. Sometimes they're with the drama club, and other times you'll find them jamming with the band. These social butterflies are rarely pinned down, navigating social spaces with an almost wizard-like grace. It's a superpower of sorts to be able to dance through the hallways without being caught in the fiery crossfire of gossip and social faux pas. I'm convinced they have a secret map of the school that dictates the safest routes to avoid any awkward encounters.

Let's not forget the emotional swings that come with these dynamics! Friendships can flourish in seconds and then implode just as quickly over a simple misunderstanding, like who got the last piece of celery at the salad bar at lunch. One moment, it's all cuddles and giggles, and the next, it turns into an Oscar-worthy performance of betrayal and drama straight out of "The Bachelorette." There's an unspoken rule that emotions run high and fall low, all while trying to maintain a carefully curated online persona. They live in fear of a screen-shot or being "unfollowed" on Instagram - cue the collective groans of betrayal!

As a teacher, I find myself wandering through this minefield of teenage emotions like a bewildered tourist in a foreign land. I try to maintain my composure while simultaneously suppressing laughter at their dramatic antics. There's always a lesson hidden within their social exchanges, often delivered with the theatrical flair of a Broadway star. It's no wonder I always find humor in the chaos, considering that one can only survive in this world by dishing out just the right amount of wit and sarcasm.

Yes, the social dynamics of teens are like an elaborate dance. It feels like one part foxtrot, three parts chicken dance, and a whole lot of shuffling out the way when the drama unfolds. At

the end of the day, these interactions teach resilience, adaptability, and of course, invaluable lessons in navigating the twisted
ways of human relationships. Give it a few years, and they will
look back on it all with a mixture of hilarity and horror, and
most likely give a collective sigh of relief that it's over. Until then,
I'll be here armed with snacks and a million dad jokes, navigating this jungle with them. After all, someone's got to keep the
peace (and the chips on hand for emotional support)!

COMMUNICATION BREAKDOWN

Communication-the elusive art that has baffled humans since the dawn of time. It's like trying to find a parking spot at the mall during the holiday season: just when you think you've got it down, the universe throws a curveball and sends you spiraling into chaos. In the realm of teenagers, effective communication feels like attempting to decode hieroglyphics from the comfort of a rollercoaster. Every day, I step into my classroom ready to unravel the puzzles these kids present, only to find that their mastery of communication is on par with an international game of charades-lots of mimes, exaggerated gestures, and the occasional accidental slap to the face.

At the heart of this breakdown lies the technological avalanche that has buried real-life conversational skills under endless scrolling on social media. Let me tell you, texting has changed the game! I can barely get my students to respond verbally, but send them a message on Snapchat, and it's like I've activated their superpowers. Suddenly, they're channeling their inner Shakespeare through a series of emojis and a slew of abbreviations that could stump even the most seasoned text translator. "LOL, BRB, SMH"-it's all a delightful alphabet soup where I can't help but wonder if they're actually chatting or secretly planning an escape from math class!

What's even more entertaining is the context behind these messages. For example, if a student texts "K," I can practically feel the gravitational pull of existential dread emanating from their very soul. Was it meant to symbolize "okay"? Or is it an indication that a life-altering event has just taken place, like the wrong flavor of Gatorade being handed out at gym class? The ambiguity is staggering, and as an educator, I often find myself standing on the metaphorical sidelines, scratching my head. "Okay? K? Are we celebrating? Or should I bring them a comfort snack?"

As I attempt to bridge this communication gap, I often remind my students of the power of face-to-face conversations - the ancient, nearly forgotten art of uttering actual words in real time. But let's be honest, watching them get flustered in a one-on-one interaction is like witnessing a puppy attempt to climb a staircase for the first time: adorably awkward with an occasional tumble. Eye contact? Forget it! Getting them to look up from their phones is like asking them to complete a triathlon. We must develop our real-world skills, my dear students! It's time to trade in those thumbs texting for some harnessed vocal cords.

Then, there's the delightful challenge of language. Each year, I find myself inundated with an influx of new slang that makes the Tower of Babel look like a friendly neighborhood coffee shop. Gone are the days of calling someone a "dude" or "pal";

now, they've stepped it up to "lit"{which can either mean exciting or just average) and "bet" {which may or may not involve wagering). I've lost count of how many times I've had to don my linguistic detective hat. Is "goat" the four-legged animal, or are we talking about "greatest of all time"? Who knew I'd be navigating the tightrope of teenage verbiage while simultaneously attempting to teach English?

On the bright side, social media does provide a convenient platform for communication, where the art of a killer meme reigns supreme. These kids can express more with a single image than I can with an entire essay. The problem arises, however, when the lines between virtual interactions and real-life experiences blur so significantly that they can't distinguish between the two. I constantly have to remind them that firing off a GIF in the middle of a serious conversation is not exactly a recipe for success. "Look, kids, memes are great and all but unless you're getting an award for 'Best Supporting GIF,' maybe save them for group chats? Thanks!"

This is why humor finds its way into my teaching style-laughter is the best icebreaker. When I can lighten the mood, students are far more likely to crack, open up, and communicate honestly. I often find myself quipping that communication breakdowns are a chance for life to remind us that we're not in a sitcom where every zinger lands perfectly. Instead, we navigate our clumsy conversations in the unpredictable world of high school, like trying to ride a unicycle on a tightrope - challenging, messy, and always more fun with a comedic twist!

At the end of the day, communication, or the absolute lack thereof, captures the beautiful, chaotic essence of teenage life. It's a puzzle that slowly pieces itself together, one awkward encounter at a time. In the classroom, we create a safe space for trial and error, encouraging anyone to embrace their inner eloquence or misstep with a hearty laugh. Because when it comes down to it, in the world of teenagers, if you can survive the communication breakdowns with your sanity intact, you deserve a medal - or at least a slice of pizza. I know what I'm getting at the next faculty potluck!

THE INFLUENCE OF TECHNOLOGY

Technology-the double-edged sword of the 21st century! In the hands of teens, it's both a blessing and hilarious source of chaos, like a mischievous gremlin unleashed in a candy factory. On one hand, this digital wonderland is undeniably a powerhouse of knowledge; on the other, it's a wild ride filled with distractions that can send even the most motivated student spiraling into the black hole dance videos. As a retired police officer turned educator, I find myself watching my students navigate this digital minefield with equal parts, admiration, and utter disbelief, like I'm witnessing a magic show where the magician accidentally reveals every trick.

Let's start with the incredible access to information! With a few deft swipes of their finger, my students can access more knowledge than the entirety of the Library of Alexandria-assuming they actually bother to type in a search term that isn't "Who wore it better: Kardashians or royalty?" Here they are, standing at the precipice of the digital age, armed with a device that can pull up a lecture on quantum physics or reveal the most efficient way to make slime. If only I could figure out how to channel that enthusiasm into their educational pursuits, we'd have the next generation of Einsteins at our disposal!

Unfortunately, what often manifests is a head-spinning permutations of distractions. Sure, they can conveniently look up answers to algebra problems, yet their fingers seem to have a mind of their own, leading them down a rabbit hole of cat videos, conspiracy theories, and, of course, that relentless cycle of social media updates. It makes me wonder - how can they learn anything when their attention is bouncing off the walls like a pinball in an old arcade machine? I've tried to capture their attention with lectures that rival TED Talks, only to have their gazes vanish into the depths of their screens as they intently investigate whether lunch is better than brunch.

Social media has certainly changed the game in ways I never anticipated. It's like having a particularly chatty parrot in the room - loud, colorful, and occasionally spewing random nonsense. For my students, social media is where friendships are forged, disputes are aired, and the whirlwind of their social lives unfolds. I can't tell you how many times I've heard someone say, "I broke up with him on Snapchat," as if announcing a royal decree. It's as if relationships have been reduced to a series of emojis and filters, leading me to ponder whether future relation-ship therapists will specialize in decoding teenagers' social media feeds instead of engaging in traditional counseling. You've got to appreciate the creativity that technology has unleashed, though.

However, there are some rather curious side effects. When I ask my students to create a simple presentation on a topic, some choose to present their findings using the latest video editing software, while others opt for an elaborate Instagram page that would require an entire team of graphic designers to pull off. Sometimes, I just want to yell, "Kids! You can't simply re-create the Sistine Chapel as a Snapchat story. This is a PowerPoint for crying out loud!"

And let's not overlook the curious phenomenon of "information overload." With such constant access, every "newsflash" seems to carry the weight of a presidential address. My students are bombarded with headlines ranging from the profound to the ludicrous - "Scientists Discover a New Planet!" to "Man Eats 50 Bean Burritos in One Sitting!" It's enough to make their heads spin! I often remind them that not everything on the internet is true and that some viral videos were indeed the outcomes of questionable decisions and lack of well-placed insurance. There's a fine line between "stay informed" and "stay mentally unhinged"!

Privacy has taken on a whole new meaning in this technology-driven realm. Sharing personal experiences online can quickly spiral into public spectacles. I've watched friendships fracture over questionable posts and seen the drama unfold that rivals the best movie plots. In my classroom, I often jokingly assert, "If it's on the internet, it's official! Just think of it as your new biography!" The students either crack up or look genuinely horrified at the thought of their embarrassing moments becoming perennial highlights.

In summary, while technology has transformed the landscape of learning, it's also set the stage for more than a few absurd spectacles. As I guide my students through navigating this beautifully chaotic online world, I appreciate the endless humor and creativity they bring to everything, even if it often leaves me wondering if I've unwittingly signed up for a comedy show rather than a serious discussion about academic integrity! So, as we embark on this digital journey together, let's keep our eyes open, fingers crossed, and a healthy supply of snacks at the ready, just in case we need to fuel up to fend off an unexpected TikTok binge!

RECOGNIZING SIGNS OF DISTRESS

Recognizing signs of distress in teenagers is like trying to locate the elusive needle in a haystack. As an educator who has navigated this wild terrain, I've developed a sixth sense for spotting distress signals. It's practically a superpower at this point! A furrowed brow here, a sudden absence of enthusiasm there, and before you know it, the alarm bells are ringing in my head like I'm the overzealous security detail at a celebrity event. This is not just about being the "funny teacher" in the room; it's about being the ultimate emotional detective in the high-stakes world of adolescence.

Now, the first clue that catches my attention is often the "disappearance act." One day, a vibrant student is full of energy and quick-witted comebacks - playing the role of class clown, triggering instruments of chaos and laughter as if auditioning for a leading role on Broadway. The next day? Poof! They've vanished, leaving behind only a pile of homework and a trail of crumpled snack wrappers. It's as if they've taken the express train to the land of Melancholia. If a once chipper student starts slipping into the shadows, it's like a proverbial red flag just waved at me artistically-"Time to investigate! Something's amiss!"

Alongside this, I've noticed a common trend where stress manifests in the body. In the world of teenagers, it can bubble up in ways reminiscent of a volcano-the facial expressions of annoyance or discomfort are dead giveaways. Suddenly, a perfectly calm face transforms into one that looks as if they've just witnessed an alien invasion while solving a complex calculus problem. Fidgeting, tapping feet, or the peculiar habit of picking at imaginary lint becomes their new form of communication. I often joke that they're auditioning for a part in "Dancing with the Stars" without even realizing it! These physical manifestations make me want to jump in and say, "Hey! Let's talk. I promise not to sign you up for the next talent show." Then there are the classic signs of academic slip-ups.

A once stellar student spiraling into an abyss of missing assignments and grades plummeting faster than their morale at midnight after a Netflix binge. When a student who used to excel suddenly starts handing in work that resembles a hastily written grocery list more than an academic paper, you know you've got a situation on your hands. So, I take a moment to reach out, my humor often disguising the seriousness beneath. "Remember that time you got a 98% and I had to pick my jaw off the floor? Let's avoid a classic 40% flop this time, alright?" It's all about making the connection that they're still valued and that we can tackle things together.

Let's not forget the wondrous realm of social interactions! A teen who used to light up the room might suddenly go dark, refusing to engage in conversations or exhibiting signs of withdrawal faster than you can say "homework." It's like watching a superhero slowly lose their powers. Friendships crumble and drama ensues as they grapple with the complexities of social life, and I find myself channeling my inner therapist. "Hey, what's up? You're looking more cryptic than a fortune cookie at a bad Chinese buffet. Let's break it down over lunch!" After all, some stress management can occur over pizza, and I'm always up for blending learning with food.

Mood swings are another telltale indicator - those wild swings that could rival the most dramatic Broadway show. One moment they're ecstatic, reciting the latest TikTok trend; then next, they're teetering on the edge of despair over a homework assignment. It's enough to keep even the most seasoned teacher on their toes. When I see what looks like an emotional roller-coaster in progress, I know it's my cue to step in. "It seems like something's bugging you. Want to channel that energy into something productive, like finding a way to rationalize that math problem?"

Finally, there's the mysterious phenomenon of sudden bursts of creativity accompanied by distress. You'll find a teenager doodling furiously in their notebook or composing an angst-ridden ballad when inspiration strikes like lightning. As they pour their frustrations onto paper, I recognize this is more than mere artistry - it's a way for them to grapple with the chaos. I can't help but lean in, cracking jokes about becoming a muse. "Careful! Before you know it, you'll start charging me for life advice!"

In conclusion, recognizing the signs of distress in teenagers is an essential skill that combines keen observation with a hefty dose of humor. By staying attuned to their shifts in mood, energy, and enthusiasm for life, we can build the bridges necessary to facilitate understanding and connection. After all, sometimes all a teenager needs to navigate through the stormy seas of adolescence is a warm smile, a cheeky grin, and an adult willing to embark on this zany adventure with them! So, here's to being vigilant, humorous, and always ready for the next dramatic twist - because, let's be real, high school is nothing if not a riveting episode from the never-ending soap opera called life!

PART THREE
BUILDING TRUST IN THE HALLWAYS

THE IMPORTANCE OF BUILDING RELATIONSHIPS

Relationships! Just like a good pair of handcuffs: when they're well-made, hey hold everything together, but when they're loose, they fall apart faster than a student's excuse for missing homework. Let me take you on a journey through the corridors of high school where building relationships is as vital as remembering where you left your coffee mug - which is often in the staff lounge, surrounded by a cracked "World's Best Teacher" mug.

First off, let's be clear: students are like cats. You can't just expect them to curl up on your lap and purr (or perhaps meow their discontent) because you handed them a syllabus on the first day. No, no, my dear aspiring educational leaders! You have to earn their trust and respect. Think of it as a game of poker; the more they see your hand, the more secure they'll feel about joining the table. By showing them you're human - even if you sometimes wear a badge - students begin to drop their defenses. They start to realize you're not just the warden of knowledge;

you're their partner in this chaotic dance we call high school education.

On my classroom wall I have a quote that goes a little something like this, "If you start by focusing on student well-being and making kids feel seen, you're going to see academics and a positive classroom culture thrive. Relationships are the foundation for making school a place where all students can be successful". I've learned, through my retired cop experience, that the best way to build rapport is through consistency. You need to show up every day like clockwork. Not like the unpredictable late-night pizza delivery guy - sure, he might have the best pepperoni in town, but he's still going to leave you high and dry when it comes to your 3 AM cravings! The same principle applies to your presence in the classroom. Once students know they can rely on you, they begin to open up. Show up, share a laugh, and for crying out loud, remember to smile! It's shocking how a simple grin can slice through the most hardened hearts.

Another piece of advice? Use humor! Nothing will break the ice like a well-timed dad joke or an awkward pun. Hell, some of my finest moments in teaching have been when I tripped over the same desk that took me down during police training. Laughter is a universal language, and when students see you can laugh at yourself, they might just let down their emotional walls. Trust me, nothing solidifies a bond more than obnoxious laughter at your own expense, especially when it's equal parts genuine and cringe-worthy.

Just remember, a well-placed joke can turn a frustrating moment into a shared experience, and that's pure gold in the world of high school. Sometimes we have to sit and listen. I learned in police work that some people just need to vent. They say we were born with one mouth and two ears for a reason. We need to listen twice as much as we talk. The fact is, we don't know what a student is going thorough outside of school. Monday morning is going to be that time to listen.

I start every class, every day, by gathering the kids around the table and we talk. We talk about anything and everything. This is one of the times I make myself available to listen. Do not underestimate the strength of active listening. It may not sound as thrilling as arresting a runaway car thief, but let me tell you, there's power in being truly present when a student spills their heart out about balancing schoolwork, friendships, and whatever's trending on TikTok these days. When students feel heard they know they are being valued. They unleash a torrent of thoughts, hopes, and even gossip about who was caught burning tacos in the microwave during math class. These small moments allow you to create deeper, more meaningful bonds that well-serve the educational journey.

And hey, let's not forget that building relationships is a two-way street. My students were and still are very curious about my life asa retired cop. One of the very first lessons I taught on reading comprehension was an old police report (with names and personal info changed of course) on a drug arrest I made. Before I even got into the second paragraph, every student had their hand up with a question. Then we acted out the traffic stop. This lesson was the foundation of the relationships I currently have with my students.

I have to give credit to one of the best teachers in my school. This man is the teacher that if you ask any student who their favorite teacher was in high school, they would say his name. Now I won't put his name out there because he already knows this, but he has been the inspiration for a lot of the teachers at the high school. The relationships he's built are a direct result of the success he's had in the classroom. He's a teacher that is always open to learning and never forgets he's a student himself. So, Mr. R, keep doing your thing! A Forensic Science class is exactly what students need to help them consider a unique and challenging career.

Keep pushing forward my friend and keep your head on a swivel! 10-7 So with that being said share some stories! Who cares if it's not what the principal or another teacher may do. Who cares if the learning target isn't part of the curriculum. The most unorthodox lessons can be exactly what you need to set the pace for the rest of your life with those students. Now just remember that we don't want the "shock and awe" reaction type of lesson, but rather the moments of challenge, perseverance, and even humor. Let them see that you're not just living in a classroom bubble. Evidence shows that authenticity invites trust. So next time you leave your coffee cup on your desk, let it serve as a reminder to be real; because students will pick up on dishonesty faster than a rumor spreads through a high school.

Ultimately, building relationships in the classroom is not some mystical phenomenon - it's simply a commitment to being there for your students. It's a willingness to make "invested time" your new best friend. Sure, you might get a few wrong turns along the way, but those missteps can lead to the most meaningful triumphs. Just remember, every moment spent building connections is an investment in that student's future - a future that may very well not involve handcuffs... unless they're a future police officer! So, grab your metaphorical friendship handcuffs (the softer, nicer kind) and get to work. You might just find that forging relationships will help you tackle the madness of high school with a smile on your face and maybe even a few new friends along the way.

ACTIVE LISTENING TECHNIQUES

Active listening! The magical art of paying attention. It sounds simple, right? But let me tell you, my friends, learning to listen actively is like training a cat to fetch: it's a challenge, and there's a solid chance you'll end up as the punchline in your own story. So, grab a chair, maybe a stress ball (you'll need it), and let's dive into the thrilling world of listening like your very job depends on it. Spoiler alert: it does!

Active listening is not just a fancy term thrown around at teacher training seminars to dazzle your peers. It's about making a genuine effort to hear what our students are saying, even if they sometimes say it in the vague language of teenage poetry or a flurry of TikTok references. When you tune in, fully, it's like you've turned on the Wi-Fi signal in a world of dial-up modem connections. Your students will feel that immediate boost in signal strength, enabling them to communicate more effectively - less buffering, more connection!

First things first, put down the grading papers and ditch the distractions. Just like you wouldn't try to foil a thief while eating a pint of Ben &Jerry's (trust me, it won't end well), you can't listen properly if you're preoccupied with your phone or planning your next lesson. If someone comes to chat, drop everything - no halfhearted nods while your eyes are glued to your screen like a raccoon to a shiny object. Instead, demonstrate that their words hold weight. It's time to channel your inner detective. Lean in, maintain eye contact, and maybe even tilt your head like a German Shepherd named Atlas when you hear them talk about that ultra-dramatic breakup or their pet goldfish's secret life.

Next, and this is crucial, use verbal and non-verbal cues. Do you know those nods and "mmhmm's" that you hear at the dentist while they scrape your teeth? Think of it as the hallmark of good listening, minus the threat of a root canal. While a student spills their emotional guts about their math test - gone - wrong or the drama of getting stuck in a locker (yes, it happens), nod along, throw in some "I see" and "go on." Give them space to finish their thoughts without feeling rushed. If you start interrupting like a rude game show host, they'll clam up faster than a cat in a room full of vacuum cleaners.

But let's not forget the art of mirroring. No, I'm not talking about that awkward high school dance where everyone stomped around, trying to mirror each other's questionable moves. This is different. When they express something significant, reflect back on what you've heard. For example, if a student says, "I just can't handle all the pressure from my teachers," you can respond with, "So you're feeling overwhelmed with everything that's expected of you?" (And yes, this is a great time to check your own level of pressure-induced snacking too!). This not only confirms that you heard them - it also gives them the green light to delve deeper.

Of course, emotions run high in high school, which means that sometimes, feelings are raw and conversations can get heated. If a student comes to you absolutely fuming, don't panic! Like a police officer trained to handle a riot at a town hall meeting, take a deep breath (preferably not in that "please don't crowd the donut tray" way) and remain calm. Acknowledge their feelings without adding fuel to the fire. "I can see that you're really upset. Let's talk about this." Those few words can diffuse a situation faster than a fire alarm in a popcorn factory. Recognizing their frustration opens the door for healing through discussion instead of chaos.

Remember, active listening is not only about hearing words but understanding the non-verbal signs that accompany those words. Look out for facial expressions and body language, and trust me, read the room. If a student walks in wearing sunglasses indoors, you may want to address the elephant in the room - or at least inquire why they believe they're an undercover celebrity. Their silence can speak volumes, whether it's showing discomfort or representing a deeper issue, understanding those signs can help foster trust and connection.

In the end, the golden rule of active listening is about respect and being present for our students. They spend hours dealing with homework, social drama, and the critical decision of which TikTok dance they need to master next. By implementing these techniques in the classroom, you not only refine your skills as an educator but also empower your students to express themselves. When they feel heard, well, my friends, they might just discover they have a whole lot to say - and who wouldn't want to possess a little more understanding of the magnificent mess that is teenage life? Now, if you'll excuse me, I have to return to the world of grading... or should I say, my never-ending quest for more coffee.

CONNECTING THROUGH SHARED INTERESTS

Connecting through shared interests - a fancy way of saying, "Hey, let's find something we can both bond over before I have to chase another kid through the halls like it's a scene from a poorly written action movie." It's the secret sauce to transforming your classroom from a stuffy dungeon of despair into a vibrant haven where both teachers and students thrive. Not only does it build relationships, but it also crafts a learning environment that's so engaging even the most apathetic teen will think twice before asking if they can go to the bathroom for the third time in a single class.

Now, let me tell you something crucial: When you walk into a room filled with students, you are often met with the daunting yet fascinating world of teenage interests. They can range from the latest pop sensation to a previously - unknown underground hobby that usually involves knitting outfits for their pet hamster. Whatever the case may be, finding something you can both relate to is like trying to find Waldo in a field of identical striped shirts - but trust me, it's worth it!

Consider this: you've stumbled upon a student who passionately talks about video games. Ah, video games - a realm where imaginary worlds are built and destroyed faster than you can say "take your hat off." Use that golden nugget of shared interest to connect! Slip in a comment about how you once tried to survive the pixelated apocalypse in "Pac-Man" or how your attempt at "Call of Duty" ended with a hole in the wall and a family pet confused about who you are cussing at. Suddenly, you are not just a teacher; you're a comrade in a pixelated universe. This newfound relationship fosters an atmosphere where students feel safe to express their thoughts, ideas, and mischievous plans.

Not to mention, those situations spiral into your chance to teach invaluable lessons. Imagine one enthusiastic gamer sharing tips on getting through a level and then connecting that back to problem-solving skills in math - Oh boy! You've now linked fractions to defeating dragons, and trust me, no student wants to miss that kind of magical connection. They might even see math as something other than a method for making their heads spin like they just got hit by a rogue taki chip.

And let's not forget about pop culture - the rich tapestry of references that students layer their conversations with like toppings on a pizza. From facebook to viral memes - connecting through shared cultural touchstones can create instant camaraderie. Just last week, I found myself discussing the merits of "Cops" with a group of students. That's right, folks! With just one well-placed "That's what she said," I had them laughing and instantly saw their walls begin to crumble, brick by brick.

But it's not just pop culture and gaming that bond us -

shared interests also extend into sports, crafts, and hobbies. If you notice a student with a skateboard, dive into the daredevil world of wheel-grinding tricks and nearly - there wipeouts. Or take a moment to unearth the artistic talent of the budding Picasso who draws on anything that doesn't move. Finding common ground in art could transform a dreaded lecture into a spirited conversation. And don't underestimate the laughs you can share over their abstract interpretations of math concepts!

Another vital aspect of connecting through shared interests is embracing the power of curiosity. Ask students to share their latest obsessions, whether it's the intricacies of anime storylines or the death-defying art of competitive eating. At times, their eyes may widen as they realize a teacher is not just a soulless bag of rules and deadlines, but rather a fellow human being with opinions, laughter, and maybe even some embarrassing moments.

Admittedly, there will be times when interacting with students centers around interests you'd likely never venture toward alone. There I was, trying to wrap my fragile brain around Roblox fandoms where fandom names resemble secret elite societies. But there's beauty in that chaos! By embracing these avenues of dialogue, you instill a sense of curiosity and openness in them, and that's what really matters.

In conclusion, connecting through shared interests is not just a pleasant endeavor, it's a necessity for cultivating a rich classroom culture. By tapping into the things that excite our students, we make learning enjoyable and foster genuine human connections.

So, grab that skateboard, research your way into the Roblox phenomenon, or reminisce about that time you couldn't beat your nephew at "Super Mario Bros." Through shared interests, we engage authentically, slice through the teenage angst, and collectively pave the way for a classroom where learning thrives. Now, where did I put my "cool teacher" hat? Maybe I'll just decorate my bald head instead, mind you, wasn't bald when I started at the high school!

CREATING TRUST THROUGH CONSISTENCY

Creating trust through consistency is a bit like laying down a thick concrete sidewalk: it takes time, patience, and probably a little sweat - and let's be honest, a few minor injuries. That's right, trust doesn't just sprout overnight like the dandelions in my backyard. It builds up gradually, one interaction (or footstep) at a time. In my experience as a teacher and former law enforcement officer, I've learned that students flourish in environments where they know what to expect, which is funny considering how often their own behavior resembles that of caffeinated squirrels. A little consistency goes a long way, my friends!

Imagine walking into the classroom and transforming into a reliable presence in an often unpredictable world. When students enter your room, they should feel the vibes of Ah, my teacher is here, and everything's chill." Whether it's at the beginning of class, during lunch, or in the midst of an emotional meltdown over a midterm, being a steady influence provides students with a safety net in which they can take risks, learn, and grow without worrying that you're suddenly going to switch into strict mode faster than a teacher during Finals week. It's like being the calm before the storm - or rather, the calm during the student's latest existential crisis over the correct use of "there," "their," and "they're." News break! If your students email you when you are not in school that day, you're on the right path.

Now, building that trust involves maintaining a predictable routine. Seriously, routines are like the warm embrace of a well-worn hoodie on a chilly day; they make life feel secure. Routine may be the saving grace for a student with ADHD, but as teachers, we cannot accept the word routine. In both law enforcement and teaching, routine doesn't exist. No matter how much you plan or train, the reality is that nothing goes as planned. Both professions require the ability to think on your feet and adapt as curve balls are being thrown at you. One way to set student routines is to set clear expectations right from day one. Create daily schedules that might include listening to a few puns from yours truly (trust me, they'll get groan-worthy), reviewing the syllabus, and establishing ground rules. By outlining what students can expect, they have the comfort of knowing that you're guiding them through the chaotic wilderness of high school one pun at a time - like a GPS for the emotional road trip of adolescence.

Consistency in communication is also key. You need to keep your promise of showing up for one-on-one conversations, attending school events, or even returning to your classroom during lunch to help that kid who's convinced they can only write poetry while sitting on a beanbag. Your moments of engagement, like a fire alarm in a school, can have profound effects on student lives. If they see that you follow through, this builds the bedrock of trust, and suddenly, they're more willing to approach you when they need help. Just watch out for that one kid who thinks the only way to ask for help is by accidentally knocking over a stack of textbooks.

Next, let's chat about feedback! Nothing screams "trustworthy adult" quite like providing consistent and constructive feedback. Instead of sending grades like mysterious envelopes from Hogwarts, make space for conversations and personalized attention. Utilizing rubrics or clearly defined grading criteria sends the message that you're not just throwing darts at a wall filled with student assignments to determine their fate. Give them specific, actionable feedback, and trust me, it'll encourage them to grow and improve rather than turn in the same sad excuse for an essay titled, "Why My Dog Ate My Homework" that we all secretly dread reading.

However, no one is perfect - not even your favorite teacher, whom they inexplicably decided to dub "the legend" during a Snapchat rant. You might even have missed a deadline or inadvertently made that little smart aleck spill his drink in a fit of laughter after a particularly embarrassing joke. The trick here is to own up to your mistakes and show yourself to be learnable (yes, I'm making up words now). Admit that you dropped the ball, just like that time I forgot a student's birthday-don't worry, they made sure I wouldn't make the same mistake again by writing it on your office whiteboard. This approach empowers students to see that everyone, even adults, can stumble.

In the end, consistency isn't just about rigidity; it's about being that beacon of trust in the ever-changing life of a teenager. By establishing predictable routines, offering consistent communication, and awning your imperfections, you create a fertile ground for trust to flourish. It's like being the steady rock in a sea of teenage turbulence, guiding those little ships to shore while they figure out how to sail. We are not all in the same boat. We are all in the same storm with different boats and you will have some students with no boat at all. Be the one who rescues those students and bring them aboard yours.

So, folks, let's keep laying that concrete sidewalk and show our students they can count on us to be there - through thick and thin, through the bubbles of laughter and the occasional chaos. Who knows? You might even discover that genuineness and consistency will help build some mighty bridges over the rocky waters of adolescence. Now, who's up for another cup of coffee while I contemplate my next classroom pun?

OVERCOMING BARRIERS TO BUILDING TRUST

Overcoming barriers to building trust is a lot like trying to navigate a minefield while carrying a stack of textbooks and a heart full of hope. Spoiler alert: it's complex. But fear not, my friends! With the right strategies and a hearty sense of humor, we can not only traverse this chaotic landscape but will also turn it into a teaching moment about the importance of resilience - because what else screams "high school experience" like learning how to dodge obstacles?

First off, we must contend with the uniting force of fear. Ah, fear - the most insidious barrier of them all. It lurks in the shadows like that one questionable piece of cafeteria food you dare not touch. Students can come to class carrying a backpack filled not just with textbooks but also with the weight of expectations, anxiety about grades, and sometimes a fear of being rejected by their peers. How can we expect them to build trust with us while they're busy wrestling their internal monsters? To cut through this thick cloud of trepidation, we need to create an environment as cozy as an inflatable pool filled with marshmallows (not that I'd know why you'd want that *wink*). Encourage open conversations where students can share their fears without judgment. Your classroom should be a safe haven, not a high-pressure plant nursery where everyone feels like they're competing for sunlight.

While we're at it, let's address the elephant in the room: previous experiences with authority figures. Now, I know what you're thinking - surely, *their* past teachers weren't as great as me, right? Well, unfortunately, not every teacher has the same rockstar status. Students often walk in expecting teachers to either be policy enforcers or overly nerdy figures that only reference outdated pop culture. Building trust means showing students they're dealing with a real, relatable human being, preferably someone who can pull off both wisdom and a truly awful dad joke without breaking a sweat. Share a little of your story, like how you once tripped and fell after writing a traffic citation or how you were caught with a cliff hanger in your nose and didn't find it until the end of the day.

Then we have cultural barriers. Schools today are melting pots of backgrounds, beliefs, and traditions-sort of like a culinary experiment gone wonderfully right. However, these differences can sometimes create misunderstandings. My advice? Embrace the diversity in your classroom like you would embrace a giant teddy bear at a discount store-enthusiastically! Take the initiative to learn about your students' backgrounds and interests. Attempting to understand their cultures and values not only builds bridges, but it also communicates respect and shows that you genuinely care. A student from a Hispanic background might prefer discussions around their family's traditions rather than being quizzed on conjugating verbs, and *boom*, just like that, you've made an ally in class. Let's not overlook the role of communication barriers!

With a group of teenagers, you face a unique concoction of language that 1) defies all humanity, 2) complete ambivalence to discussions, and 3) the occasional overwhelming medium that is... silence. Yes, silence! Have you ever confronted that stillness in a class where you passionately ask a thought-provoking question and all you get is a chorus of crickets? The solution here is to leverage multiple forms of communication. Introduce group work, technology, and even one-on-one discussions to create dialogue that resonates with students. Power up that classroom technology! Make amusing video snippets, utilize social media for positive interactions, or even conduct debates on TikTok trends. You may just find that shy student who stares at their shoes will share the most profound insights once you channel their energy into a medium they're comfortable with.

Lastly, let's talk logistics. The world outside of school can be equally turbulent and chaotic, and that chaos doesn't vanish after the welcome bell rings. Family dynamics, socioeconomic status, and external pressures all contribute to barriers that can impede trust-building. Acknowledging students' realities is vital. From that last-minute request for an extension on a project because their dog ate their homework (which might be true!) to understanding how plate spinning at home translates to academic performance - we must adapt. Providing additional resources, being flexible with deadlines, and having candid conversations about their challenges can help each student feel seen and respected. After all, we are not just educators; we are advocates in their corner, championing their journey through the stormy seas of adolescence.

At the end of the day, overcoming the barriers to building

trust is about showing vulnerability and honoring the shared experience of learning. So, let's embrace the chaos, anticipate the hurdles, and lead our students toward a future filled with laughter, learning, and relationships that last - because if we can't weather the storm together, what's the point of standing outside in the rain when there's a perfectly good umbrella of connection waiting to be shared? Now, I think there's a cup of coffee with my name on it. Time to get ready for round two!

PART FOUR
CONFLICT RESOLUTION 101

UNDERSTANDING THE NATURE OF CONFLICTS AMONG STUDENTS

When I transitioned from wearing handcuffs on my duty belt to wielding a yard stick in the classroom, I quickly learned that mediating student conflicts is a lot like stepping into a high-stakes game of chess - only the pieces are half-baked potatoes, and the rules are written in invisible ink. Conflicts among students can erupt over the silliest of things: who got the better piece of pizza at lunch, who borrowed whose homework, and who is dating who? But these seemingly trivial issues are often more complex than they appear. Understanding the nature of these conflicts not only helps in managing them but also provides insight into the social dynamics that dictate life inside the colorful chaos of a high school.

Picture an average high school hallway during the passing period. Imagine a scene that's equal parts chaotic and comedic students dodging students like they're in a high-octane action film, backpacks swinging like medieval maces ready to take out any unsuspecting victim. In that frenzy, it may look like madness, but there's a strategy at play. Whether it's establishing social hierarchy or simply claiming the territory around the coveted vending machine, students are constantly navigating a world that's precariously balanced on the brink of hilarity and hostility. Conflicts arise out of that navigation - a simple misstep can lead to a verbal confrontation or, worse, a captive audience of bewildered teachers.

As someone who spent years in law enforcement, I can't help but notice how many situations are similar to crowd control at a rock concert - everyone is amped up, filled with hormones and nacho related energy, and navigating which group gets to stand by the water fountain. Often, a conflict is a case of miscommunication or misinterpretation, where one student thinks another is staring too long at their lunch, thereby declaring it war on their personal turf. Navigating this social jungle without letting the drama escalate is a professional skill in itself. As a teacher, my duty isn't just to stand idly by; I need to interpret and intervene effectively, diffusing situations before they resemble an episode of a reality TV show.

In another light, we need to consider the unspoken rules of "he-said-she-said." School is a social laboratory, and students are the woefully undereducated lab rats. They get caught up in twisted narratives and exaggerated stories faster than you can say "detention." What starts as a mild disagreement can balloon into a full-blown tale of betrayal, resulting in alliances that resemble the political parties of the show Survivor. Everyone wants to be involved in the latest feud, and before you know it, an innocent exchange over pencils has spiraled into an elaborate social debacle.

Then there's the issue of identity. In a world where teenagers are defining themselves against a backdrop of memes and hashtags, a conflict over something like a 'cool' sweater becomes a battleground for self-worth and social standing. Students feel they must defend their reputations with the ferocity of a lion protecting its cubs. However, these so-called battles can sometimes feel like wars over the last slice of pizza. But connect the dots, and you'll find that the stakes feel monumentally higher to the students. If only they knew that in the adult world, pizza remains a perennial issue - albeit one that gets solved with a simple, "You can have that slice, I'll just have a salad."

Recognizing these layers of conflict is not about assigning blame or creating hierarchies of victimhood. It's akin to being a referee in a game where all players have wildly different playbooks. As educators, our role is to shine a light on these conflicts with understanding and humor, occasionally wielding the metaphorical whistle to help students navigate their differences. We must show them that while their problems feel like the most significant global dilemmas, they can approach resolution with the same finesse as a well-timed punchline.

At the end of the day, the nature of conflicts among students is an insightful glimpse into adolescent society. It's filled with drama, humor, and an artful blend of misunderstandings and miscommunications. As I dust off my badge from the police force and strap on my teaching cape, I remind myself that while I may not have all the answers, the journey of understanding these conflicts is half the fun. I mean who can resist that kind of classroom chaos?

IDENTIFYING TRIGGERS: WHAT SETS OFF SCHOOLYARD TIFFS?

The art of identifying triggers! It's like trying to find a needle in a haystack - maddening, amusing, and a tad disheartening when you realize the needle probably disappeared in the ocean of hay. But in the chaotic ecosystem of high school, pinpointing what sets off schoolyard tiffs is crucial for us educators. Picture it as detective work: I'm donning my metaphorical Sherlock hat and magnifying glass, delving into the minds of students to uncover the mysteries of adolescence. And what I find is bewildering.

First and foremost, we have the classic trigger of territory. Teenagers may act as though they are free from the primal instincts of our cave-dwelling ancestors yet watching them hang near their "spot" at the cafeteria table reveals a raw, unfiltered version of human nature. God forbid someone encroaches upon their chosen throne! It's as if one student sitting too close to another's fries has set off a chain reaction that would make a game of Jenga look like child's play. Suddenly, you have a situation: voices escalate, and what started as a simple lunch becomes a fierce debate in personal space, launching subtle insults that are as biting as yesterday's cold meatloaf.

Then there's the issue of social standing. Imagine navigating the maze of popularity among adolescents! A friend of mine, who is a former special education teacher, once explained that high school is a giant social chessboard, and teenagers believe they must make the right moves to avoid falling to their demise. Simple misjudgments or mistaken identities-like who wore what outfit during last Friday's pep rally-can provoke feuds that would throw even the finest of reality TV spin-offs into deep cries of "THIS IS DRAMA!" Students can become their own detectives piecing together clues about each other's lives to crush perceived rivals, so even outfits can turn from stylish to scandalous in seconds. Who knew that a crisp white shirt could start a brawl?

Of course, we must talk about the giants of perception-the almighty rumors. Ah, yes, these golden nuggets of overheard gossip can transform faster than my morning coffee goes cold. A whispered word here, an exaggerated tale there, and suddenly you've got conflict brewing that's more volatile than a science experiment gone awry. Students are like rumor-spreading ninjas, capable of turning the tiniest offense - a missed "like" on asocial media post-into a full-on saga of betrayal and indigna-tion. The rumor can spread like wildfire, fueled by concocted plots, conspiracies, and leaks, resulting in students declaring themselves the defenders of their truth against the "evil villain," a.k.a. their former best friend.

But let's not forget about the culture of competition that fuels these schoolyard skirmishes. Sports, grades, and anything remotely tied to who possesses the edge in a perpetual game of "Can you top this?" Competitions can morph from friendly banter to a war of egos quicker than you can say "scoreboard." Take basketball practice, for example. It's not just about scoring points; it's about scoring points with their peers and solidifying their position on the social hierarchy. A single missed shot can shatter an ego and ignite a chain reaction of insults chat can echo through the gymnasium like end-of-the-year awards.

Now, let's touch on triggers that transcend actual events and delve into the realm of perceptions and feelings. Emotions run high among these budding adults. Stress from homework, navigating relationships, and dealing with the rollercoaster ride of hormones, can lead to students projecting their frustrations onto their peers. One clumsy remark based on a bad day could unexpectedly lead to a staggering exchange of hurtful words. Adulthood may seem light years away for students, but their ability to angst - as they expertly frame any social hiccup in the world of shattering tragedy - reveals that they are all too ready to wage war over feelings that are less about the event and more about their emotional state.

Understanding these triggers allow us, as educators, to intervene preemptively before the drama unfolds into a Shakespearean tragedy on the schoolyard stage. To be a successful teacher, I need to maintain a sense of humor mixed with empathy. It's not enough to just grin and bear it when students spar over trivialities; the key is to recognize the absurdity and diffuse the situation before one of the combatants locks the other in a figurative headlock. By creating an environment where students feel safe to express their concerns and learn to communicate without the drama, we might even turn potential schoolyard tiffs into opportunities for growth.

Navigating the triggers of conflicts in schools, as complex as it may be, is all part of the grand adventure of teaching.

Embracing the ridiculousness while enlightening the minds of our students is a dance worth learning - preferably one in which no one steps on their toes or throws a milk carton in your direction. Who knew the lesson plan for life would include the fine art of schoolyard peacekeeping? Well, to paraphrase a wise teacher: "A peaceful school is a happy school - and bonus points if you can get them to laugh along the way!"

DE-ESCALATION TECHNIQUES: KEEPING IT COOL WHEN TEMPERS FLARE

The fine art of de-escalation! It's a skill akin to being a lion tamer in a circus-only the lions are fueled up on teenage angst, and the chairs you're using to keep them at bay are made of flimsy cafeteria plastic. In the high-stakes environment of high school, tempers can flare at any moment over the most mundane issues. Did someone steal the last piece of celery from the lunch line? Who dared to question the validity of a TikTok trend? Why did "he" say "she" was texting "that guy"? The trivial absurdities that ignite passionate bouts of disagreement are like dangling strings, and I'm here to be the puppet master pulling them back into line. So, let me share some tried-and-true techniques that I've picked up along the way to keep it cool when tensions rise.

First, I must emphasize the importance of maintaining a cool demeanor. I always make a mental note to channel my inner Zen master or a Yoga instructor. Walking into the scene of a boiling conflict, I visualize myself as the eye of a hurricane, calm and collected while chaos swirls around me. Taking deep breaths and projecting a soothing vibe can often help the students reset their own emotional engines. "Hey, I see you're both feeling a bit heated right now. Let's take a second to catch our breaths," is my go-to phrase. Feel free to offer an even cooler rendition - with some mild kung fu motions thrown in if you're feeling particularly ambitious! It becomes a metaphorical pause button that allows students to refocus their scattered sentiments before launching into an all-out verbal melee.

Next, I've found that using humor is like sprinkling fairy dust on a largely volatile conflict. We humans share a unique bond over laughter - it can diffuse tension faster than a school vending machine processing requests for snacks. When two students are inches away from launching into an impromptu debate on who ate the last granola bar, throwing out a lighthearted joke like, "It's not called snack warfare; it's more like the Battle of the Century: in one comer, we have John the Granola Monster and in the other, Gary the Cookie Monster. This encourages laughter and often shifts the mood entirely. Engaging their sense of humor opens the door to humility and can turn fierce rivals into eventual allies.

Another effective technique is to create space in the conversation. intervening in a dispute, I've learned the value of redirecting the dialogue away from the immediate conflict. Rather than simply asking, "Why did you hit him with your lunchbox?", I ask them to share their side of the story. In doing this, I'm creating an avenue for them to express their feelings rather than turning it into a courtroom drama. I become a sounding board for them to air their grievances, which flushes out the real issues that may lie beneath the surface level. Often, students will find that their reasons for argument stem from misunderstandings or that silly rumors have ballooned into monstrous accusations.

Eye contact is another crucial element. While this may sound straightforward, maintaining eye contact can come across as an unfiltered superpower. When emotions spike, you'll often see students looking anywhere but at each other, which only further stokes the flames. So, I ensure that I establish and maintain eye contact when de-escalating a situation, creating a safe space that encourages honest dialogue. But I also apply this superpower sparingly-you don't want to channel the icy glare of a hawk watching its prey either. Achieving the balance of inviting empathy while simultaneously signaling that I'm not interested in letting the fire grow is key, and my goal is to get them to meet in the middle with a less aggressive stance.

Lastly, allowing a cooling-off period is sometimes all it takes to put out the proverbial flame. When the heat rises and emotions are taut, the best response can be simple: give them space. Designating a short timeout - where students can take a breather, perhaps in opposite corners of the classroom or outside under the sun - can lead to quieter minds and less heightened emotions. While they cool down, perhaps encourage a brief mindfulness exercise or even a 'who can balance a book on their head' contest. I mean, after all, what place presents a perfect opportunity for a few more laughs while allowing tension to fade?

Mastering de-escalation techniques in a school environment is as much an art as it is a skill. It requires patience, humor, and plenty of practice if you are to be successful at it. Watching students evolve from furious to forgiving can be quite fulfilling, especially when you compare their previous state to a lion about to roar. When armed with these techniques, I navigate those charged moments with a smile, content in knowing that I'm not just mediating conflicts; I'm planting the seeds for a resolution, teaching mindfulness, and basking in the sweet glow of teenage chaos. If all else fails, a bazooka of ice-cold soda can go a long way in bridging differences. Let's face it: we might not achieve world peace in a schoolyard, but we can at least keep it cooler than a popsicle on a summer day!

FROM THE POLICE ACADEMY TO THE CLASSROOM: PRACTICAL TIPS FOR TEACHERS

As I transferred my skills from the Police Academy and sixteen years on the force to the classroom, I imagined my first-day jitters not as a typical teacher would, but as a former cop. I had an extensive collection of crazy stories about the wild antics of criminals. Picture this: I stride through those school doors in my best "cool teacher" outfit - faded jeans, a vintage rock band T-shirt, and of course, a trusty whistle hanging around my neck. But the reality quickly hit me that while I could handle unruly citizens with a firm voice and witty banter, managing a classroom of hyperactive teens would require a different arsenal of practical skills and a fair amount of patience. So, let's dive into what I learned as I blended my cop instincts with teaching smarts.

First off, let's tackle the importance of presence. In the police world, it's essential to command attention-students are not that different. This resonance, the aura of "I'm in charge, but I'm also here to help," is crucial. Picture yourself walking into a room with a confident strut. In class, this translates to what I like to call the "leadership stance." Shoulders back, a smile ready to launch, and a quick scan of the room brings a sense of energy and establishes that I mean business. Students pick up on this energy; a confident teacher can set the tone better than the loudest whistle. My years on the force taught me the power of non-verbal cues, and oddly enough, flashing that "I'm here to guide, not to hammer!" smile can crush the most daunting of tensions.

Then there's the magic of communication. One of the most powerful tools in any teacher's belt - whether you're patrolling the streets or managing a classroom lies in effective communication. In law enforcement, we learn quickly that verbal skills can de-escalate fiery encounters, and the same applies to teaching. I have discovered that some students thrive on banter, while others prefer a sweeter, gentler approach. Tactful questioning rules the day in controversies, leading with "What do you think about...?" instead of "Why did you do that?" just might save me from a great explosion of teenage sass. When students feel heard and understood, the lines of communication open wider, creating the foundation for a richer learning experience. And let's be real; knowing when to inject light-hearted humor can bridge any gap faster than I can say "Stay in your lane!" during a traffic stop.

Now, let's pivot to consistency and structure. Anyone who has been in law enforcement knows that rules provide clarity. If one could envision a classroom as a miniature police district with its own codes and laws, then the same principles apply. Establishing consistent rules and structure from the get-go allows students to understand expectations, just like a new recruit learns the ins and outs of police protocol. I've learned that the best way to achieve this is through consistency, not with the heavy-handed approach of a traffic enforcer. Instead, I lay out clear expectations for behavior, engage students in developing a classroom contract, and try to establish an open-door policy so that expectations are not just laid down like a police sergeant barking orders. This collaboration empowers them, creating a sense of ownership over our classroom universe.

Two words: Active listening. I know we have already talked about this, but we have to engage both hearts and ears. This may sound like a cliché, but those who survived the Police Academy know the immense value of listening to all stakeholders involved. From complaints about too much homework, to grievances on inedible lunch options, students need to feel respected and validated through active listening. Ready to jot down notes and nod encouragingly, I make it my personal mission to employ everything I have stored in my heart, from graceful ears to genuine concern. Building relationships stems from knowing their lives, so when I see "normal" teen issues, I relate them back to the classic games of cops and robbers that led to minor altercations - not to the extended jail sentences I used to hand out.

In the end, transitioning from the Police Academy to the classroom taught me valuable techniques that can transform an ordinary teacher into someone students admire and respect. Strategies built on presence, communication, structure, active listening, and relationship-building pave the way for an engaging and harmonious classroom experience. Just like in law enforcement, it's all about the interactions we cultivate and the energy we bring. So, the next time I step into that classroom ready to shape young minds, I'll remember that even in the world of education, I can blast through the barriers with humor, connection, and just a sprinkle of police-inspired magic to keep it lively!

ENCOURAGING OPEN DIALOGUE: FOSTERING COMMUNICATION SKILLS IN STUDENTS

When it comes to encouraging open dialogue in the classroom, it's like playing the world's largest game of verbal Leapfrog-students and teachers hopping over the various hurdles of hesitation until we land gracefully in the lush pastures of confident communication. My years both as a police officer and now a special education teacher have taught me that effective communication isn't merely about exchanging words; it's about connecting, empathizing, and yes, even throwing in some of that priceless humor. So, grab your imaginary or real-speaking megaphone because we're diving deep into the art of fostering communication skills amongst our future leaders and entrepreneurs!

The first step in this verbal adventure is establishing a safe and welcoming environment. Much like a squad car needs a sturdy frame to withstand the chases, my classroom detours must feel like a fortress of trust. My approach revolves around letting students know that they can express their thoughts and ideas without fear of judgment or ridicule. I often start class with a light-hearted icebreaker - "If you had to share a secret skill, would it be more embarrassing to know how to do a TikTok dance or beat-boxing?" Setting the tone that our classroom is like a confident spandex suit: flexible, comfortable, and, most importantly, not designed to criticize. Gradually, students warm up, sharing snippets of their day and cluing each other into their tastes, interests, and hidden talents.

Once the magical ambiance of openness is swirling around us, I actively encourage my students to practice communication techniques through structured dialogues. Think of it as the Olympic Games of Classroom Conversations. At the start, I introduce basic frameworks like the "Agree-Disagree-Take on a Position" format, nudging students to build arguments while considering their classmates' perspectives. "Alright folks, I need your best debate faces on! You've got 30 seconds to convince me whether pineapple belongs on pizza!" The thrill ignites, and before we know it, we've sprinted past opinions to explore our differences while laughing at the absurdity of arguing over toppings in the first place.

One of my favorite tools for cultivating these conversational skills is the buddy system! Pair students up or create small groups regularly to explore topics together and share their perspectives, all while creating a stimulating and dynamic environment. This allows students to practice articulating thoughts with small support systems, lessening the trepidation tied to larger class discussions. I often say, "Your opinions matter in this classroom, but when I say buddy up, I mean it - NO secret groups allowed, and definitely no overcooked burritos being thrown!" The laughter often breaks the ice, and soon, students grasp the value of discussing a range of topics, from serious issues to which superhero deserves to be on the top of the 'most powerful' list.

Now let's get real, sometimes students need a gentle nudge to break through those sticky walls of hesitation. To address this, I incorporate dramatic activities where they "act" as someone else for the class. "Today, you'll be channeling your inner news anchor!" I might exclaim, and soon, my students adopt roles that help them flex their vocal muscles. Whether they're delivering a whimsical news report on the latest cafeteria scandal or interviewing their classmates on the hot-button topic of fashion Ugg boots, they quickly realize that communication thrives when you step outside your comfort zone. Watching their faces light up as they master the art of asking questions is an especially joyful sight.

Recognizing that listening is equally as essential as speaking, I commonly introduce listening exercises that foster empathy and compassion. "Alright, team, half the class will share their thoughts while the other half nods in attentive argument like you've been struck by the beauty of that riveting story." It's a playful take, but it reinforces that listening is an active sport, not just a passive one. The more we practice being attentive readers of our peers' body language, infections, and emotions, the deeper the connections become.

I also understand the importance of feedback in honing these skills. After engaging in discussions, I make it a habit to encourage self-reflection.

"How did it feel to share your ideas today?" or "Did you learn anything new from your peers?" By integrating constructive feedback, students can evaluate their communication styles and recognize their strengths while also pinpointing growth areas. Approaching weaknesses with humor often allows for that delicate balance; rather than fearing critiques, they learn to embrace the learning journeys that come with mistakes.

Encouraging open dialogue transcends mere skill-building; it cultivates a sense of belonging and respect within the classroom. So whether I'm polishing the gleam of my duty boots, or aiding a dreamy student facing a world of silent judgments, I know every conversation leads us closer to dismantling barriers. Fostering communication skills prepares them not just for academic success, but for navigating the complexities of adulthood in a connected world. So in the spirited atmosphere of my classroom, with laughter echoing through the walls and camaraderie blossoming among students, I embrace my role as a facilitator of conversation, confident that with a dash of vulnerability and a sprinkle of wit, the possibilities for meaningful dialogue are endless!

PART FIVE
NAVIGATING THE SCHOOL SYSTEM

UNDERSTANDING THE SCHOOL HIERARCHY

The school hierarchy - a structure so complex it could rival the plot of a soap opera. As a retired cop and special education teacher, I'm pretty familiar with hierarchies: give me a police precinct or a school hallway, and suddenly it's all about the pecking order. That's why it's crucial to understand the different layers of authority in a school setting. Let's break it down like an McHammer song!

First up, you've got the Big Cheese, the principal. Now, I'll tell you, these people often strut around like they own the place, and in many ways, they kind of do. They have the authority to hand down decisions that could make your life easier or turn it into a scenario reminiscent of a horror film. In many ways, they are like the ultimate drivers of the school bus. They steer the ship, decide which way to turn, and occasionally swerve to avoid curricular potholes. The lesson here is simple: keep them on your side. I'm not saying you have to like them or go have a drink after school, but a friendly wave in the hallway or a "great job last week" can go a long way.

Like in law enforcement, administrators come and go. Best case scenario you end up with a genuine leader. Hopefully you get someone who not only steers the ship but provides support to their teachers and puts those teachers first. I have worked for people who have no clue what it means to lead. Bad leadership leads to a high turnover rate, destroyed morale, stressed employees, and poor performance. Principals go to leadership trainings three times a year and retain nothing. They then strut around even more because they went to leadership training and think they are now an expert. The fact is, good employees don't leave because of bad jobs, they leave because of bad leadership. When good employees who have been in their jobs for decades start leaving, then someone needs to start asking questions. Remember, like any good cop would tell you, leadership isn't about experience or years of service. It's about building trust and confidence. Ask yourself, if the boss blows the battle horn, would you follow him into that battle. If the answer is no, then you my friends don't have a leader.

Next in line are the assistant principals. These educators are the building deputies riding shotgun. They help keep everything in check and might even be the ones who have to change their way of leading because of the principal. Having worked side by side with these folks, I can tell you that they wield significant power, and their office doubles as both a disciplinary center and a support service for various teachers. It's their job to enforce rules without turning the place into a penal colony. If your assistant principals have been there long that the principal, more than likely they feel the same way you do about the boss who micromanages everything. You could say they're tasked with relaying the "bad news" all the while trying to maintain order. If you don't like the principal, keep your assistant principal relationship a priority. It may be your only lifeline.

What about the teachers? Ah, yes, here's where it gets interesting. Each teacher thinks they reign in their classroom kingdom, yet they're often caught up in a continual power struggle. This is often with the students, who try to establish dominance. Now toss in a little friendly competition like teacher of the month awards, the "best lesson" badge, and those awesomeness awards from the district office and you have a recipe for chaos. So, here's my suggestion: align your weapons, I mean strategies with your fellow teachers. Keep alliances strong; a well-prepared team can tackle anything from a surprise fire drill to the latest school policy changes. Keep your peers close and on the same page. Whether it be to participate in a petition to fire your bully principal or for support in handling a student, you will need your allies at some point down the road.

Here comes the fun part: the students. Contrary to what you might think, they're the wild cards. In this hierarchy, they're the unpredictable element that can turn a perfectly planned lesson into a one-way ticket to chaos. But, as any good educator knows, understanding the student population well is key. Spend some time getting to know their social structures: the cliques, the rebels, the class clowns, and the overachievers. This social maze can serve as a treasure map-not for gold, but rather for student engagement and classroom management. Give them respect, and they'll often surprise you with their ability to thrive and contribute positively to the dynamic of the class.

But wait, there's more! In the backdrop of this whole dysfunctional circus are the support staff - the unsung heroes of the school system. Custodians, cafeteria workers, counselors, and aides, these individuals have insights into the school hierarchy that you wouldn't believe. Want to know which students are getting extra attention or are likely to be a handful? They know. Want to score some delectable snacks for an impromptu party? The cafeteria staff might help you out - be nice, and they might just share the secret stash of brownies. So, next time you think hierarchy is just an administrative framework, remember to tap into these expert resources who can make or break your teaching experience in unexpected ways. On our special education team, our paraprofessionals are life savers. They have a very difficult job and yet they show up, give 110%, and take on some of our toughest students. Our jobs would be a disaster if our paras were not there. So to all the paraprofessionals out there, thank you for your dedication and hard work. None of it goes unnoticed.

Understanding the school hierarchy isn't just a roadmap; it's a strategy. Navigate your way through this ecosystem like you're a seasoned cop strolling through a familiar neighborhood. Recognize the roles of everyone involved, leverage your relationships and you might just thrive as the coolest teacher on the block. And if you do it right, maybe -just maybe- you can convince the principal to actually cover your class when you have an IEP meeting (Yea don't hold your breath).

KEY POLICIES IMPACTING STUDENTS

Key policies impacting students are like the fine print on a contract - nobody reads them until chaos ensues. As a retired cop who now teaches special education, trust me when I say that if you don't know your policies, you might as well hand in your badge and sit in the corner of the room Policies are the invisible forces that govern a school, shaping everything from curriculum to behavior, and, let's be honest, they sometimes feel like they exist solely to drive teachers - especially my fellow veteran law enforcement-turned-educators- absolutely bonkers.

Let's start with the big one: discipline policies. Every school has its own set of rules, usually crafted with the utmost care and forethought, more realistically, hastily thrown together during an espresso-fueled faculty meeting at the end of the school year. Some schools endorse a "restorative justice" approach, where misbehaving students are ushered to soothing circles of dialogue rather than facing consequences.

These policies are often put in place with no discussion

involving the teachers who are expected to enforce the policies. The problem lies in the administrators going to the wonderful seminars over the summer listening to presenters who have never taught in a classroom, yet they educate administrators on things they can throw into a policy. Well administrators, I hate to break it to you, but those ideas may or may not work at your school. If you want to bring back some new ideas, talk to your teachers before implementing those ideas. If you want to destroy the morale in a school of great teachers, that's the way to do it. Having 80 teachers on the "this is the stupidest thing I've ever heard" side of the policy, is not how you want the school year to start.

Speaking of drama, let's dive into that lovely mix called inclusivity policies. You'd expect this to be a good thing; the more the merrier, right? Well, when policies designed to include everyone turns into a free-for-all where students think they can just saunter in and out as they please, the classroom can feel like a zoo rather than a learning environment. It is more than likely the awesome new rule (and yes that's sarcasm) the principal came up with that is causing the zoo like environment.

In wrapping up our whirlwind tour of key policies impacting students, remember this: they can feel like the ultimate labyrinth. While they are put in place to provide structure to what can often resemble a chaotic circus of teen drama and educational pursuits, if you want to keep your job, it's crucial to approach them with a mix of understanding, humor, and a certain level of fierce determination. After all, navigating these policies might not always be rewarding, but with a little bit of wit and occasional eye-rolling, we can certainly make the bumpy ride significantly more entertaining!

THE ROLE OF ADMINISTRATION IN STUDENT SUCCESS

Administration-where the magic happens, or so they say. As a retired police officer turned teacher, I've had the privilege (or sometimes the pleasure) of witnessing firsthand the ever-enigmatic role that administration plays in the wild world of student success. Forget about superheroes; if you really want to know who swoops in to save the day when students are struggling, all you have to do is look toward the office for encouragement and guidance. Administrators should know that the dynamics of the classroom can shift faster than a high school senior's mood after a long day. Part of an administrator's job is to help teachers navigate challenging dynamics by providing professional development opportunities, classroom support, and useful advice. Sadly, this doesn't happen as much as it should. If the teachers are overwhelmed with the phenomena of "what do I do with a classroom where all the students are, let's say, being less than cooperative?", then the administrators should be part of the solution, not part of the problem.

Let's take a moment to appreciate the delicate balance they perform in managing discipline. As much as we want to believe that all students are on the path to enlightenment and self-discovery, the sad truth is that a few of them seem determined to test the limits of our patience - daily. Administrators can play a pivotal role in addressing behavioral issues. This is done by working with teachers to enact appropriate discipline while ensuring due process is upheld. Their ability to handle these sometimes-tumultuous situations can greatly influence the classroom vibe and dictate how students perceive authority in educational settings. Remember though, administrators who have to intervene could make things worse. You must think long and hard if you want to risk that outcome.

Lastly, let's not underestimate their role in engaging with the community. Our schools exist within a larger social context, and successful administrations know that to create a thriving educational experience, they must partner with families and local organizations. Much like your favorite local diner dishing out homemade comfort food, the best admin teams cater to the needs of students and parents alike. By working collaboratively to create outreach programs, informational seminars, or just fun community events, they foster an environment supportive of student success beyond the walls of the classroom.

In conclusion, the role of administration in student success is multifaceted and undeniably important. They are the behind-the-scenes magicians, juggling budget sheets and grant applications, working tirelessly to ensure that students receive the best possible experience. While many may view administration as a distant presence, the truth is that their influence permeates through every crevice of our educational system.

If you have a supportive administrative then having them on

call may be beneficial. If you have an administration full of managers who has a reputation on making things worse, then you may want to lean on peers to help with strategies and suggestions. While I can appreciate the intent of fostering understanding, let's face it: sometimes a time-out just doesn't cut it. Students need to learn that actions have consequences. Sure, we want to encourage empathy and communication, but handing out hugs instead of detentions? Playing patty cake in the counselor's office to resolve an argument just isn't going to cut it. It just might lead to more chaos than calm.

Next up, attendance policies. You would think these would be straightforward-show up to class, done deal. But oh no, fellow educators, these policies can be a tangled web of absences, tardies, and excuses that make you feel like you're wrestling with a python. We've all seen or heard of students crafting elaborate stories to escape the clutches of a mandatory attendance policy. "My dog ate my homework, and then I had to take him to the vet for a rabid squirrel bite" only captures part of the creativity I witness daily. Look, I'm all for acknowledging absences due to legitimate issues, but if we don't establish clear boundaries, the attendance rate around here could rival the attendance at a staff Christmas party.

Let's throw in the cake icing-academic policies. These range from grading systems to graduation requirements, and I'm telling you, they can feel like navigating a minefield. In my previous life in law enforcement, the rules were somewhat clear-cut; if you break them, expect a visit with a badge-wielding offi-cer. In education, grading can be a subjective experience filled with the complexities of student competency, parental pressure, and those ever-present "I didn't know this was due" excuses that can unleash a tidal wave of angst. Finding that delicate balance between holding students accountable while fostering a culture of growth can require a level of diplomacy worthy of international negotiations. Remember we are teaching life skills and responsibility. The goal is to teach the students to be successful and hold themselves accountable in the real world. This is not middle school anymore. Time to shit or got off the pot.

Now, let's not forget about the ever-important special education policies. I've stepped into this arena after swapping my police badge for a teaching badge, and let me tell you, the policies here can be a wild ride. From IEPs (Individualized Education Plans) to 504 Plans, these aren't just mildly inconvenient paperwork, they are legal documents. What's the fun in having a policy if you don't have the possibility of being sued?

Special education teachers play by a different set of rules. Our students are unique and are all on a different path to the finish line. Policies that are put in place sometimes contradict IEP accommodations and goals. The fact is that all students, not just special ed students, learn differently. That's why with special ed students have an IEP. We are trained differently and see academics in a different light. These kids don't have grades, they have goals. If an emotional behavior support kid has a goal to manage anger a certain way, then putting that goal to work in the classroom is a great way to helping that student deal with behavior. If it's not used, then why is it in the IEP. We are trained in how to implement these goals. Hopefully as they navigate their high school years, they learn strategies to handle their behavior in the real world.

Let's now transition and talk about the big-picture thinkers-the administrators who plot the course of the educational ship. With their gaze pointed firmly at the long-term goals of student success, they have to map out educational strategies that cater to an ever-changing student demographic. Their plans often resemble a magician's performance: one moment, they announce a grand initiative designed to improve test scores, and poof! They vanish amidst a cloud of fragmented departmental responsibilities, teacher angst, and let's be honest, over-whelming amounts of data analysis. I mean, it's astounding that they can keep track of all that, while simultaneously main-taining a mostly pleasant demeanor. Ever tried smiling while in your mind you're deciding if that one teacher really has your back? Yeah, it's like that.

Now, the real task for these administrators is to create a learning environment where our future leaders can thrive. That means ensuring resources are available - not just the textbooks gathering dust in the corner of the supply closet. They are tasked with the Herculean challenge of securing funding for programs that resonate with today's students. Picture them as the school's grant- and funding-soliciting ninjas, out there in the world hustling for technology, sports equipment, or the latest in educational wizardry. Their ability to procure resources plays a crucial role in elevating student success. Let's face it: your department can put in the request for these valuable items, but in my experience, the ball is always dropped by someone, and you'll never get what you asked for. There may be administrators out there who get shit done, but you need to know your admin if you're going to put in for that request.

But wait! There's more! Another critical aspect of the admin-istration's involvement in student success is their role in teacher support. Teachers are like the front-line soldiers fighting the daily battle of education, but where do these brave souls go when they're in need of backup? You guessed it - the administration. Teachers rely on their admin partners to create a culture of collaboration, support, and professionalism.

When the support you need doesn't make itself known, you catch yourself questioning the enigmatic antics of your administration. Now remember that they're likely doing their best to create the perfect storm of resources, support, and community engagement. If there's one thing, we all know, in a school setting, chaos is always just one unsupervised hallway away!

NAVIGATING SPECIAL EDUCATION LAWS

Navigating special education laws is like swimming with sharks dressed in business suits; it's a daunting task, and unless you know what you're doing, you might find yourself taking a bite out of more than you bargained for. As a retired cop turned special education teacher, I can assure you that laws and regulations governing special education are meant to be protective and supportive, but sometimes they feel more like a marathon through a maze. So, grab your map, it's time to plunge into the intricacies of this world. First up, let's set the record straight: the Individuals with Disabilities Education Act (IDEA) is the big kahuna in special education law. Think of it as the ultimate rulebook. Passed before many of my students were born, IDEA mandates that every child with a disability has a right to a free and appropriate education. It's a noble concept, but the fine print often makes you question who wrote it. The law insists that students must be educated in the least restrictive environment possible, which is essentially lawyer-speak for "let's not lock them away in a room and throw away the key." Instead, we favor inclusion. However, navigating how to actually implement this can feel like assembling IKEA furniture while blindfolded. You're left wondering, "Is this an 'A' or a 'B'? No, wait - where does this even fit?"

While IDEA sets the tone, there's also a laundry list of regulations that come along for the ride. Did you know there's an entire repository of acronyms that are like the secret handshake among special educators? IEP, FAPE, LRE, BIP-if acronyms were currency, I'd be rolling in dough! Individualized Education Plans (IEPs) are developed for students with disabilities, and they're as crucial as the planning period you desperately need before a four-hour faculty meeting. Every IEP includes measurable academic and functional goals tailored to the student. But be warned; crafting an IEP can sometimes feel like you're trying to pull teeth - with little to no anesthetic. Balance the student's specific needs with parental expectations and educational standards, and you're in for a real wild ride, friends.

Now, let's throw into the mix that IEP meetings can be akin to family reunions on steroids. You've got administrators, general educators, parents, and sometimes even the students themselves-each person bringing their own set of hopes and desires to the table. Picture it: about as calm as a stampede of wild horses with the collected knowledge of a hundred parenting books thrown into the fray. Then, of course, there's the annual review of the IEP-it's like a birthday party you're forced to attend every year, full of delicious cake but sprinkled with anxiety. You'll be questioned about how Johnny's "emotional regulation goals" turned from "calm during math class" to "in the neighbor's yard building a sandcastle" in mere weeks.

Let's also discuss the Americans with Disabilities Act (ADA), which expands on these rights and ensures that students with disabilities aren't discriminated against in public education. The ADA can be like that enthusiastic friend who shows up at your party uninvited but means well. It requires schools to make reasonable accommodations, which sounds great until you realize that "reasonable" is a subjective concept. For example, in a world where providing extra time on tests or allowing assistive technology seems second nature, there's still that one teacher who might insist on correcting every student's grammar in "text" speak. Trust me, your job is to teach them, not to play grammar police; they shouldn't be judged on whether they're "LOL" or "BRB" proficient.

Another thing worth noting is the role of Behavior Intervention Plans (BIPs). If you thought the IEP meetings were chaotic, welcome to the circus of BIPs! These documents focus specifically on improving challenging behaviors - not unlike a plan devised by a police officer trying to handle a criminal mischief call making a group of teenagers do community service. While they are absolutely necessary for some students, the implementation can be messy. Once you start trying to use behavioral goals and strategies with the flexibility of a pretzel, ideally, the whole thing could spiral into complete pandemonium - especially when kids react in unexpected ways. One moment, you're actively promoting a soothing bubble wrap popping session, and the next thing you know, they're akin to a superhero, ready to take down anything in their path.

In the end, navigating special education laws is a journey that can often feel like an obstacle course designed by a group of overly caffeinated lawmakers who've never set foot in a classroom. But with persistence, creativity, and a healthy dose of humor, you can advocate for your students and help them achieve the educational success they deserve. It may take more than a map but trust me: the reward of seeing a student bloom when given the proper support is worth every twist and turn along the way. So, wear your "I'm a special education ninja" badge with pride and dive headfirst into the uniquely wild world of special education law - your students are counting on you!

BUILDING RELATIONSHIPS WITH OTHER EDUCATORS

Building relationships with other educators is as essential as mastering the art of sandwich making in a cafeteria - incredibly important yet often overlooked. As a retired cop turned special education teacher, I can't stress enough the impact that camaraderie and collaboration with fellow educators can have on the overall learning environment. It's not just about sharing lesson plans and grading tips; it's about developing a network of support, inspiration, and frankly, some good old-fashioned levity in what can often feel like a pressure cooker of responsibility.

When you step into a school for the first time, it's essential to acknowledge that you've plunged into a complex social ecosystem. Picture it as a reality show set in an educational institution - everyone has their quirks, specialties, and those occasional "I-can't-believe-they-just-said-that" moments. Building relationships with other teachers swiftly should be a goal.

While we may have different approaches to our teaching

styles, we share the same vision - helping students succeed and survive the daily chaos of high school.

One of the best ways to cultivate these relationships can be accomplished through meeting during lunch, after school, or on a lunch duty assignment. I am pretty nonsocial in my school and this is by choice. I am not friends with every teacher in the school, however my team and the people I work with on a regular basis is my group. You will find during these meetings there is a lot of drama and rumor mills. Even though I realize the importance of knowing the teachers, I pick and choose who I talk to. Mybe it is my old cop attitude knowing I don't trust people and that's why I have a small circle of friends. Either way, have some friends and use that time to vent or talk shop. It's all up to you. Once you have those friends, you'll soon discover that most of your colleagues share similar frustrations; after all, misery loves company! Plus, it's a wonderful opportunity to learn from one another's experiences, swap war stories about the most bizarre student encounters, or dive into a passionate debate over which method actually works for classroom management. Trust me, there's nothing like dissecting the finer points of classroom survival tactics with a peer who's just as caffeinated and exhausted as you after a long week.

Next, don't underestimate the power of collaborative planning sessions. I quickly found that a few minds are often better than one when it comes to lesson design. Sure, I might have my own brilliant (or not so brilliant) ideas about teaching English, but bouncing those ideas off a colleague who specializes in English can elicit gems of wisdom I would have never considered. Imagine the thrill of two educators wrestling with a complex topic, throwing ideas around like pancake batter until we finally unveil the perfect recipe! It not only enhances our creative approaches but also reinforces respect for each other's areas of expertise. Trust me; laughter is the best ingredient for an engaging lesson!

Social media has further shaped how we build professional relationships in today's educational climate. In an age where hashtags reign supreme, joining online teacher communities can help narrow the gap between our classrooms. You can collaborate, share resources, and connect with like-minded educators who might be facing similar challenges.

Let's not forget about the importance of creating space for professional development- it's not just a requirement, but an opportunity to seize the day! Workshops, conferences, and trainings provide beautiful occasions to rub elbows with fellow educators and dive deep into subject areas we might not engage with regularly. These events often feel like adult field trips but with an added agenda. While that agenda may sometimes feature an overwhelming number of PowerPoint slides, you can also discover a wealth of creative strategies to bring back to your classroom.

My advice? Always have a snack ready. It fosters not only survival but an "I've got your back!" spirit that brings educators closer.

Of course, communication is key to maintaining strong relationships with other educators. Whether it's shooting a quick email for assistance, engaging in a friendly chat during passing periods, or making time for informal coffee meetups, these little gestures can go a long way. Building trust within our professional peer group leads to enhanced collaboration and an unspoken commitment to support one another whenever the going gets tough.

In conclusion, building relationships with fellow educators

is an essential investment in your teaching journey. Emphasis should be placed on collaboration, humor, and camaraderie, as these relationships can significantly impact our daily challenges and victories in the classroom. Life as an educator can feel daunting, but by standing shoulder to shoulder with our colleagues, we create a united front that not only benefits us but also resonates with our students. So, grab your lunch tray, make a few connections, dive into the chaos, and relish the wonderful bond that grows amongst educators - because together, we are mightier than any wild anecdote that could ever land in an educational handbook!

PART SIX
CREATING A SAFE SPACE

CREATING A WELCOMING ENVIRONMENT

As someone who transitioned from the world of law enforcement to special education, I quickly learned that the first step towards a successful day in the classroom is to create a welcoming environment. Just like I did in the police department squad room, I framed police patches from police departments from all over the country to remind us of that thin blue line. Yes, that's right, the intimidation tactics of my former life have no place when it comes to educating teenagers. In fact, having a smile and an open door is much more useful in the classroom than if I handcuffed my worst student and the whole class threw dry erase markers at him.

A welcoming environment starts the moment students walk into your classroom. The first rule of thumb, ditch the rigid, military-style decor. That means trading the gray concrete walls for something more inviting-think motivational posters and rules for writing essays. I aim for lively colors and a few key decorations showcasing student work, which, believe me, is like putting a Picasso next to a toddler's finger painting. But when it comes to fostering excitement about learning, it all counts!

Next up, let's talk about seating arrangements. I know what you might be thinking let's line 'em up, military-style, so they know who's in charge! If you throw students into seats like they're detainees checking in, you might as well replace the desk with a bench in a courtroom. Instead, go with a more flexible arrangement, maybe put the desks in a U-shape or divide them into small clusters. This way, students can see each other's faces rather than just the back of their classmates' heads (which, let's be honest, isn't the most inspiring view). Yes, your classroom can look more like a cozy coffee shop than a police lineup. No welcoming environment is complete without a great set of ground rules. Now, I could put up a list of dos and don'ts that could rival the Ten Commandments, but that'd be about as exciting as watching paint dry. Instead, let's make these rules catchy and easy to remember! For example, instead of "Respect your classmates and their property," I could say, "Treat classmates like your favorite video game. While we're at it, what better way to foster a sense of community than to involve students in crafting those rules together? Empowerment equals buy-in, and they get a little piece of ownership in their own learning space - no handcuffs required!

Now, again, this is the third time so far that I've talked about building relationships. By now you should realize that relationships are everything in education! On the first day of school, I tell my students, "You're going to laugh, you're going to learn, and on occasion, you might fall asleep. But that's okay! Just don't snore!" When students know I genuinely care about them, they feel safer and more comfortable, which is the secret sauce to establishing that warm and fuzzy feeling in the classroom. With some humor and a dash of heartfelt compassion, trust can blossom. After all, it's hard to be a knucklehead when you're faced with my dad jokes.

Speaking of humor, let's not forget to embrace the weird quirks of teenagers. You wouldn't force a bear to wear a tutu, right? So don't expect teens to fit into a mold of what society deems "normal" either! Celebrate individuality-encourage students to share their interests, whether it's an obsession with cats or a long-standing rivalry with a rival school's mascot. We've all been a little odd, right? I still regret wearing a 70s wig and high knee socks during a staff vs students volleyball game.

In summary, a welcoming environment is essential to creating an atmosphere where students not only feel safe but also want to excel. You might have started as a retired cop trudging into the education field, but you'll soon discover that nurturing learners is like lifting weights. It requires patience, sensible techniques, and occasionally letting their ego disappear because a 46 year old retired police officer just showed them up on the bench press. So, deck out your classroom with love, laughter, and a few dad jokes, and watch as students transform into learning machines.

ESTABLISHING GROUND RULES

Establishing ground rules in the classroom is kind of like trying to direct traffic at a five-way intersection. Everyone's going in different directions, and if you don't establish guidelines, you might end up with a traffic jam that would make any cop want to pull their hair out. From my previous life in law enforcement, I can confirm that nothing brings out chaos faster than a crowd without boundaries. And trust me, I've seen some wild stuff - like an emotional support kid barking under a desk. Teaching is as unpredictable as police work is. You never know what each new days brings.

Now, the first step to laying down the ground rules is engaging students in the process. Who says rules have to come from the teacher's judgment throne like they do in a police movie? Let's flip the script! On the first day of class, we brainstorm rules together sort of like a group therapy session, only with fewer feelings expressed and way more eye-rolling. I usually say, "Let's create some rules that would make even the strictest police chief proud!" This way, I'm not just an authoritarian overlord; I'm their partner in crime, well, not literally, of course.

As we toss around ideas, it's vital to keep the rules realistic-like "No food fights" or "Avoid wrestling matches unless it's a pre-approved MMA tournament." Recognizing that students have busy lives outside of school, I encourage them to contribute rules that accommodate their lives. They often propose ridiculous rules, like "Students should be allowed to have Wendys every Wednesday," and I pretend to consider it as I stifle a laugh and remind them that this isn't a lunchroom. Instead, we focus on fundamental concepts: respect, responsibility, and of course, a strict "no snoring unless it's during a movie day."

Once we've settled on a solid list of rules, I like to present them in a way that's memorable, like a catchy jingle. Who could forget "No phones in class, unless you're using them to flash-mob your way through a stellar math problem"? Maybe not the next Billboard hit, but it sticks. I even made a poster to display the rules.

One of the greatest parts of establishing ground rules is that it sets expectations for behavior, but it can also bring a spirited discussion. Almost like watching a courtroom drama unfold, students will petition for why "getting an automatic A on Fridays" should be an official rule. "Imagine the enthusiasm!" they'd say. I counter with, "Well, imagine the apocalypse when grades soar faster than my ego after lifting weights!" It's not just about the rules; it's about the wrestling match of ideas that helps us all come to the same page.

Once we have our rules in place, I make sure to review them

periodically, just like a cops-and-robbers rerun. Seriously, you wouldn't believe the number of times I've had to remind kids that "No running in the classroom" doesn't just apply to their feet but also to their mouths! To really hammer home the importance, I come up with fun role-playing scenarios to illustrate the rules in action. If we have a "celebration" for birthdays, the students have to practice why we can't go rogue over cupcakes. It's a light-hearted reminder, and they love it (and sometimes send me off on wild "creative" tangents).

So, to establish effective ground rules is to create a structured yet inviting classroom environment. It's a cornerstone of building relationships, creating trust, and ensuring that everyone feels they have a voice. I might be a retired cop-turned-teacher, but I assure you that I still hold the title of Chief of Classroom Shenanigans. So, let's enforce the rules together, laughing all the way to a newfound learning experience, where the only crime committed will be a little too much enthusiasm for math!

Now, it's also important to have a little fun, because let's face it: learning is hard enough as it is! In my class, we embrace the absurd, and humor plays a significant role. When students walk in, they're often greeted with a strewn mess of clever wordplay and silly props. I can't remember the last time someone danced in a courtroom, but in my classroom, we dance our way into learning! If we're discussing literature, we might enact the plot with ridiculous sound effects that would make a sound engineer cry. Yes, there's something incredibly liberating about watching students get lost in laughter while they engage with the material, and let's be honest here: laughter is an essential component of learning.

Another crucial aspect of building these positive relationships is to be there for them when the going gets tough. Life as a teenager can feel like an unyielding obstacle course, from navigating socially treacherous situations to surviving the emotional rollercoaster of finals week. I strive to cultivate an empathetic space where they can confide in me when they're feeling overwhelmed. My rule of thumb: listen with a heart and a keen sense of humor. If a student shares that they failed a math test, I might respond with, "Well, guess what? Even superheroes have off days! It's all about how you bounce back." Bringing in a positive spin can be contagious, and before long, you're left with a group of students who trust that they can tackle obstacles head-on-preferably without the use of handcuffs.

Now, I also approach my students as individuals, each with their own unique story. Just like how no two donuts in a box are the same - some glazed, some chocolate, and definitely some filled with jelly-my students come with diverse backgrounds and experiences. Embracing that diversity is vital in our learning environment. I often host events that celebrate different cultures, and it's always commendable to see how students come together to share their stories through food, music, and art. Who wouldn't want to learn about history over a plate of empanadas, or math while engaging in a spirited debate around the proper way to eat sushi?

In the end, the heart of building positive relationships is cultivating an environment where laughter, trust, and respect thrive. After all, it's not just about pouring knowledge into their heads; it's about molding individuals who feel supported and are eager to learn and succeed - hopefully without turning anything into a crime scene. Whether we're laughing at each other's missteps or supporting each other through the heavier moments, we're reminding ourselves that we're in this together. So, to all my retired cop friends looking to step into the class-room: grab your cape, because we're not just teachers - we're also mentors, cheerleaders, and, believe me, 95% of the time, the most exhausting stand-up comedians you've ever met!

INCORPORATING STUDENT VOICE

Incorporating student voice in the classroom is akin to hosting your very own TED Talk but without the fancy stage, spotlight, or cool conference swag bags. Instead, it's about creating an environment where students feel empowered to share their thoughts, ideas, and well - let's be honest - sometimes their completely outrageous opinions, which can be just as entertaining as they are insightful! When students feel like they have a seat at the table they're more engaged, more inspired, and let's face it, the classroom vibes are significantly more pleasant. Gone are the days when I could simply lecture like I was delivering a monologue in a police procedural drama.

The first step toward incorporating student voices is to genuinely invite them to share their thoughts in the classroom. This isn't about creating another bureaucratic form they must fill out, no, no! I'm talking about embracing a more dynamic approach. Every day, I dedicate a moment to what I call "The

Floor is Yours" segment. It's an open forum where students can discuss whatever is on their minds - whether it's school-related, a captivating new social media trend, or which superhero would make the best teacher. Seriously, you'd be amazed at the flame wars that ensue over whether Spider-Man or Iron Man would ace one of my tests. It's electric!

Now, understand, that this is not just me inviting them to share random, off-topic musings about their social media. We focus on relevance, somewhat. I might redirect the conversation if we veer off-course too much, because while I'm all for creativity, I don't really need to hear about the latest dog meme while we're trying to figure out literary analysis. Still, I never shy away from cracking a joke or two and taking their perspectives seriously. If a student believes they have a revolutionary idea for school lunches that involves pizza every day of the week, I'll gently remind them that potential heart attacks need to be factored in but hey, go ahead and set up that petition!

Another way I empower student voices is by incorporating choices into their learning. It's as though I'm The Genie from Aladdin - except here, I'm granting students more than just three wishes! For instance, when it comes to group projects, I allow students to choose the format whether they want to create a video, a podcast, or even a silent film where they communicate entirely through interpretive dance. Giving them options frees them to express their understanding in ways that resonate with them. Plus, it has the added bonus of sparking creativity; you might just end up with a group project that features a rap battle about photosynthesis. I'm telling you, educational gold!

Feedback is another vital component in the mosaic of student voice. Regularly checking in with students about their experiences contributes to a strong feedback loop that fosters growth. I like to call it "The Student Satisfaction Survey," which really just entails asking them two questions: "How am I doing?" and "What more can I do?" Essentially, it's like the teacher version of Yelp (minus the snarky comments). It's surprisingly eye-opening to hear how easily students can identify areas where they feel engaged compared to where they might feel like they're stuck in a time warp, listening to lectures on the life of Charles Dickens for the 245th time.

Now, look, it's not all sunshine and rainbows; sometimes, when you invite feedback, you might get a dose of reality that leaves you chuckling or sobbing into your coffee. I once received a comment saying, "I had the style of an old-timey, donut-eating cop," which wasn't entirely inaccurate. So, I embraced it! I turned that feedback into a goofy classroom activity called "Donut Discussions," where we held class conversations while enjoying donuts (who wouldn't want to learn English while munching on a sprinkle donut?). Combining humor with the lesson created a light atmosphere, and you better believe that feedback has improved since then!

Incorporating student voice is essential for fostering a thriving classroom culture. The more students feel like their voices matter, the more invested they will be in their education, ready to step outside of their comfort zones. I strive to create an atmosphere where they can bask in the full glory of unfiltered opinions, flashy creativity, and even when it veers into the absurd, an understanding that their thoughts are just as valuable as any textbook on the shelf. In the end, it's not just about teaching in the traditional sense; it's about shaping new leaders, innovators, and, most importantly, individuals who are not afraid to speak their minds. Remember, when you let students express their voices, they're more likely to end up in less trouble because from what I've seen, they have a knack for stepping behind the metaphorical police tape of relevance!

ENCOURAGING INCLUSIVITY AND RESPECT

When it comes to fostering an inclusive and respectful classroom environment, I like to think of myself as the Captain America of education, minus the super serum and chiseled abs, of course. The goal here isn't just to create a space where students come to learn, but to cultivate an environment where everyone feels valued, respected, and ready to take on the world - just with a little less drama than an Avengers movie. As a retired cop turned teacher, I firmly believe that creating such an environment is crucial for the overall growth of our students, much like a good crime drama: the best outcomes come from collaboration and understanding.

One of the first steps in encouraging inclusivity is establishing ground rules that promote respect for all. When I sit down with my students to create the guidelines for our classroom, we discuss the importance of treating each other as equals-the way I once told rookie officers to treat every citizen with dignity, whether they were at the grocery store or being apprehended for questionable decisions. The emphasis here is that we value diversity, every voice matters, every experience matters, and especially every snack choice matters. By calling attention to the differences that make us unique, we can celebrate them instead of letting them become reasons for division.

To further promote inclusivity, I strive to integrate lessons that reflect a variety of cultures, viewpoints, and experiences. Forget the traditional curriculum; I like to put in lessons that expose students to different perspectives. For instance, when discussing literature, I might throw in texts written by authors from various backgrounds because why should Shakespeare have all the fun? Nothing gets a classroom engaged quite like holding a lively debate about whether Vin Diesel or Stone-Cold Steve Austin would win in a fight.

It's equally important to address the elephant in the room: students often come from different backgrounds, each with their own experiences that shape who they are. As someone who has navigated the streets in a police car, I've seen firsthand how diverse experiences can create varying perspectives. So, tackle this head-on. In activities I create opportunities for students to share about their own cultures, whether it's through cooking days (which often lead to delightful culinary disasters) or comparing holiday traditions. Let's just say the last time we had a cultural potluck, my students learned that while I might be well versed in homework, I am decidedly not a gourmet chef. However, the laughter, shared stories, and excitement made it all worthwhile.

Another game changer in building an inclusive environment is encouraging student collaboration. I derive great joy in orchestrating group activities that require students to work together to solve problems. Picture this: you have a group of students working together to build the tallest tower using nothing but spaghetti and marshmallows. I mean, who wouldn't have fun while feverishly debating the structural integrity of their edible architecture? Through these activities, they have to communicate effectively, share their thoughts, and actively listen to one another. Before you know it, those very differences that seemed daunting, become the glue that holds their teams together.

It's also essential to model inclusivity in behavior. When a student shares an idea, I ensure to validate them, whether their thought revolves around why stray cats are missing from around the Chinese Restaurant or how to build a booger fort using popsicle sticks. I make it a point to say, "Hey, that's an excellent observation!" If students see their peers being acknowledged and respected, they are more likely to reciprocate those same sentiments. Kids tend to mimic what we model-think of it as the old "monkey see, monkey do" adage, except we're raising the bar a little higher than just throwing bananas! Now, let's not forget the importance of addressing instances of disrespect directly and promptly. I've had my fair share of disciplinary issues in the past, and as a teacher, I'm a firm believer in addressing problems rather than shoving them under the rug. So, when I encounter conflict, I tackle it with clarity and intent. A gentle reminder goes a long way, like when a student once referred to another as a "bean pole". I swiftly called a timeout on that and turned it into a lesson on recognizing individual strengths. Everyone can contribute something unique to the classroom whether it's academic prowess or clever puns about quadratic equations.

By encouraging inclusivity and respect, we equip our students with essential skills for life beyond the classroom. They learn to embrace diversity, communicate effectively, and celebrate unique perspectives, not just to fit in, but to stand out in an ever-evolving world. So, let's work together to create an atmosphere where every student feels as if they belong to a larger community, united in the pursuit of knowledge and friendship. And who knows? They may just develop superhero-like empathy skills, ready to face whatever life throws their way. After all, being supportive of one another is way cooler than fighting over pineapple on pizza!

PART SEVEN
LEADERSHIP LESSONS FROM THE FORCE

UNDERSTANDING LEADERSHIP STYLES

As a retired cop turned special education teacher, I often find myself pondering the different styles of leadership in certain professions. I have worked under a lot of terrible bosses. For the record, I don't use the word leader much in the real world. A leader is a special kind of person. Unfortunately, I have not experienced many leaders in the jobs I've had. In law enforcement, I have worked under bosses that wanted his men to fear him. He was degrading, condescending, made you feel worthless, and knew the law better than anyone else. I have also worked for incompetent bosses who didn't know their ass from a hole in the ground. I have also worked for spineless chiefs who did not stand up for his men and folded when the shit hit the fan. In hindsight as mad as it made me, I learned a lot from them. The biggest thing I learned was that if I were to ever take on a position like theirs, I would never be a boss. I would never treat my guys like they treated us. I would be that leader and wear the title with pride. Educational bosses are not that different from law enforcement bosses. But let's take a look at what kind of bosses we have in our schools.

From "I'm the boss and you're all going to do as I say" to "Let's all just hug it out and share our feelings." No matter what boss you get, everyone seems to have their own flavor of authority. Understanding these styles is crucial if you want to mix like a Starbucks Latte, instead of becoming a chunky glue of clashing personalities. So, grab a seat, preferably one that doesn't have gum stuck to it, and let's break down the delightful world of leadership styles in education.

I am going to let the following "Leadership types" use the word leadership, however if anyone has these types of qualities, they are only bosses. First up, there's the "Authoritarian Leader (boss)." I remember working for a Chief who barked orders like a drill sergeant trying to whip a group of recruits into shape. He did not care about anyone but himself. He would not take responsibility for any mistakes we made but would claim credit for all the praises that we got. This style means you lay down the law, and while it can inspire fear, it often has the emotional warmth of a wet sock. They're great at making sure things get done but may leave students feeling like they're in a prison, minus the orange jumpsuits. As tempting as it might be to encase your students in bubble wrap and direct them like a marching band, it's important to remember that they also need space to breathe.

On the other end of the spectrum, we have the "Democratic Leader (boss)," also known as the fun-loving negotiator. This is the educator who asks for input before deciding on rules and practices, often resulting in a classroom that resembles a circle of friends at a local coffee shop. While this approach can foster a sense of belonging, it can also lead to discussions that meander longer than a high school student's attention span. "So, what do you all think about a school-wide dance?" is often followed by, "Can we have it on a Wednesday at 2 PM so I can leave early?" These leaders aim to include student voices, yet sometimes they risk upsetting the delicate balance of fairy dust and order that keeps a classroom floaty and functional.

Then there's the "Transformational Leader (boss)," who swoops into the scene like the superhero you didn't know you needed. The kind who inspires students to become better versions of themselves. They often have a way of making lofty visions sound as exhilarating as a roller coaster ride, only without the threat of losing your lunch at the first drop. If you've got a group of demotivated teens who couldn't care less about their algebra homework, transformational leaders might sprinkle a little motivational glitter on them, reworking their goals to sound as appealing as a YouTube video of a cat playing the piano. However, they can easily drive students up the wall if they expect them to be inspired while also forecasting the stock market in algebra class.

Another style you'll encounter is the "Servant Leader (boss)." These are the principals busy serving others - the educator who fries up support like a cook at a diner and pairs it with under-standing and compassion. It's like making sure every student gets an extra side of fries, even if it's a bit messy. They ensure that everyone's voice is heard, and they cater to needs that students didn't even know they had. But be warned: this style might mean they spend so much time ensuring everyone is satis-fied that they forget to lead the charge, leaving students sipping on their metaphorical milkshakes while the world of education whirls around them.

And finally, there's the "Laissez-faire Leader (boss)." This sounds fancy, but it often means they're the kind of leader who prefers to kick back and let students figure things out for themselves - sort of like letting kids eat cake for breakfast and trusting that they'll make wise dietary decisions. While it promotes independence, the lack of guidance can quickly lead to chaos and confusion, akin to letting a group of squirrels run loose in the school library. "Good luck finding the right book for that report, kids!" Unfortunately, those squirrels rarely have the best intentions.

Ultimately, understanding these leadership styles helps make sense of the beauty and chaos that is education. Each one has its pros and cons, and while I've said several tongue-in-cheek things here, I've learned that no style is perfect. In practice, it's about blending elements from each style, just like mixing weird toppings on a pizza to create something surprisingly edible. And more importantly, remember to invest time in building relationships that matter. Because at the end of the day, whether you're keeping order in a classroom or resisting an attempted mutiny over pizza toppings, connection is key. After all, who wants a classroom filled with students who seem to think of you as a wet sock on a rainy day?

BUILDING TRUST TRANSPARENCY

In the high-stakes world of high school, where survival often feels akin to navigating a minefield with your shoelaces tied together, one element shines brighter than a neon sign in the middle of the night: trust. And how do we earn that trust? Spoiler alert: it involves transparency- that magical ingredient that is often elusive in a world where teenage lives are filled with secrets, from the whereabouts of their lost homework to the actual reasons why they were late to class.

First, let's clarify what I mean by transparency. No, it's not just the latest trend in non-opaque window treatments. In the education context, it means being open about your thoughts, decisions, and intentions. Think of it as giving students an all-access pass into the inner workings of your brain. They deserve to know why you employ certain policies or teaching methods, much like they'd want to know why their teachers sometimes give them homework on Fridays. When students understand the "why," they are far more likely to buy into the "what." It's like introducing them to the idea of vegetables by dousing them in chocolate sauce - they might just chew!

One method of building trust through transparency is through consistent communication. I cannot stress this enough: if your classroom is a ship, you want to be the captain who steers with a steady hand and ensures everyone aboard knows the destination. Share both successes and challenges openly. If you make a mistake -own it! When students see you being honest about your shortcomings, they might actually start to feel a little more comfortable sharing their struggles too. It creates an environment where vulnerability is welcomed, and you may just find your classroom becoming a haven of support, instead of a reality show where everyone competes to outdo one another in avoiding work while wearing the latest fashion.

Let's talk about the importance of setting clear expectations. This is where transparency becomes your trusty sidekick, rather than a shady friend lurking in the shadows with secrets. Define rules, assignments, and grading criteria upfront. Think of it as laying out the blueprint for a rollercoaster ride of twists and turns. Can students expect what exhilarating drops lie ahead? When students know what to expect, they can focus less on guessing and more on doing the work. It's like informing them that the cafeteria's mystery meat will indeed not reveal its secrets at any point before lunch. Trust builds when students realize you're upfront with them, and that you're not hiding a truckload of surprise snags in your curriculum.

Building trust through transparency also requires vulnerability on your part. I know what you're thinking: "Why would I expose my inner workings to a bunch of kids?" Well, get used to it! It's imperative to share your own experiences and make connections with students on a human level. Quite frankly, if they view you only as the teacher who used to wrestle grizzly bears in a past life (okay, I did live through a few "interesting" arrests... we can call it wrestling if you like), your mission is doomed. Share your own stories about overcoming challenges and learning bumps along the way. You just might find that students feel inspired to share their jumbles of awkwardness in return-trust me, nothing builds trust faster than mutual humility and a good laugh over someone's unfortunate haircut in middle school.

Finally, let's not forget follow through. If you pledge to create an environment of trust through transparency, you must be prepared to back it up with actions. Promise to do something, whether it's addressing a concern or implementing some new feedback, deliver on that promise. If you establish trust with a whole lot of talk and no walk, students are quick to see through the charade. Keep in mind, if you set a rule about always being available during lunch hour for extra help, you better appear with coffee and a sympathetic ear; otherwise, don't be surprised when students start referring to you as "The Great Pretender."

Building trust through transparency may seem like a daunting battle, but it's one we can win together. By being open, communicating clearly, and engaging with students as real human beings, we can create an environment where trust flourishes. And trust, dear colleagues, will be the key that unlocks the incredible potential of every student in your classroom, helping them feel more secure and motivated than ever. So, get out there, and let transparency light your path through the sometimes-murky waters of education!

EMPATHY IN LEADERSHIP

Empathy-the secret sauce that elevates mere mortals to the revered status of "great leaders." In the realm of education, where wit and wisdom collide with extreme awkwardness, empathy stands out like a unicorn in a cattle ranch. It's that magical ability to put yourself in someone else's shoes - although, let's hope those shoes aren't the notorious ones that squeak like a banshee every time you take a step. As a former police officer, I've come to realize that having empathy is like being the bouncer in a nightclub; it grants you access to a whole new level of understanding and connection that can transform your leadership style.

Now, let's paint a picture: you're standing in front of a class full of high school students. You've got the jocks frowning at their phones, the goth kids trying to channel their inner Bob Dylan, and the science nerd stringing together equations like they're looking for a date to prom. In this chaotic carnival, empathy comes into play as you try to navigate the circus. It's not enough to merely tell them to put their phones down; it's vital to understand why they're glued to those screens in the first place. Maybe one is stalking their crush on Instagram, while another feels isolated, desperately looking for connection. By tapping into your empathy, you're not just shutting down distractions-you're addressing the deep-rooted needs behind them. Who knew that a connection could be more effective than a stern look?

Empathy also means approaching your students with a sense of curiosity instead of judgment. Think of it as swapping out a pair of blinders for a wide-angle lens. For example, instead of rolling your eyes at the student who claims they "forgot" their homework yet again, dig a little deeper. Perhaps they've been dealing with personal issues or simply had a chaotic morning that rivaled an action movie. By expressing understanding instead of indignation, you build a foundation of trust. The next time they come into class, they might just bring you a story about why their pet hamster accidentally chewed through their homework. And hey, at least it's a great excuse, right? A hamster heist? That's a bestseller waiting to happen in my book!

Moreover, empathy in leadership doesn't merely benefit students; it can work wonders for teacher morale as well. A school, after all, is not just a place where students learn algebra - it's a community! And every community has its disputes, personalities, and occasional soap operas unfolding on the staff breakroom couch. As leaders, we need to practice empathy toward one another. Encourage your fellow teachers to share their challenges and triumphs. By providing a space where everyone feels comfortable sharing their experiences, you lay the groundwork for collaboration and support, making everyone feel a little less like they're running a marathon alone. Because let's face it-I don't even jog for exercise, and I definitely don't want others to feel they have to race through the day either!

Let's not forget how empathy promotes a growth mindset. When students know that teachers understand their struggles, they are far more likely to take risks in chasing after knowledge. This creates an environment where mistakes become lessons rather than failures, giving students the freedom to explore their thoughts without the hovering fear of judgment. If students can feel vulnerable enough to engage in light-hearted discussions, they will also glean educational moments from those comedy sketches gone awry.

However, let's be clear: empathy doesn't mean coddling students like they're the last cookie in the jar. We still need to hold them accountable! It's about balancing understanding with the urge to guide them back onto the path of responsibility. You can empathize with a student and still expect them to hand in their homework on time.

In conclusion, implementing empathy in leadership encourages greater engagement, belonging, and growth among students and staff alike. By fostering an empathetic culture, we enhance the connection between people in this sometimes messy, chaotic world of education. When the rug burns from all those metaphorical shoes shuffling about, we aren't simply denying the complexity of the high school experience; we're embracing it with open arms as we shuffle into another day. And remember, just a little empathy can go a long way; after all, isn't that what truly makes education magical?

DECISION-MAKING UNDER PRESSURE

Decision-making under pressure is a rite of passage that we all must endure - whether in a police chief's office or during a high school pep rally where no one knows if the mascot is a bulldog or an accidental surprise from the art department. In the hallowed hallways of education, pressure can feel as omnipresent as acne during prom season. You find yourself making choices that could either catapult your day into glory or plunge it into the depths of utter chaos. With that in mind, let's dive into the art of making those tough calls while keeping a sense of humor (because honestly, if you don't laugh, you might just end up crying, and no one wants to do that in front of their students).

First, let's discuss the environment in which these decisions take place. Remember that time when your classroom turned into a mini replica of a reality show, complete with shouting students, random food fights, and unexpected breakdancing? In moments like these, even the simplest decision-like whether to announce a pop quiz or let them out early - can feel like trying to land a plane during a thunderstorm. It's at this precise moment you must channel your inner Zen master and remember to breathe. Sometimes it helps to take a moment to analyze the chaos before leaping into action; I mean, unless we're talking about a kid running toward you with a water balloon, in which case, your only decision is to run for cover!

Next, let me introduce the idea of evaluating your resources. In law enforcement, resources were more about backup officers and tactical gear; in education, it's more like evaluating your students' emotional states, classroom dynamics, and the cookie supply in the teachers' lounge. Trust me, if you find those cookies are running low on a Thursday, your resources drastically dwindle. Assessing the available minds and levels of motivation in your classroom can inform a choice as simple as introducing more hands-on activities or adopting a more lecture-based approach. The more you know your class dynamic, the more your decisions can cater to those needs, and before you know it, you'll have raised a room full of enthusiastic learners rather than a group of indifferent students contemplating the philosophical implications of using a pencil versus a pen.

Now, let's not forget the importance of a solid foundation built on previous experiences. As a former cop, I often found myself in situations where quick thinking was paramount. That time when I forgot where I parked my cruiser due to more important matters (like saving a cat stuck in a tree while trying to look heroic) taught me valuable lessons about decision-making on the fly. When making these choices in school, reflect on past experiences. Those little moments accumulate into a reservoir of wisdom, giving you the strength to tackle tough decisions head-on while resisting the urge to bury your head in the nearest desk.

The aspect of collaboration also plays a significant role in decision-making under pressure. No one is a superhero, and if anyone claims to be one, they probably shouldn't be leading a classroom. Seek support among fellow teachers; collaboration can spark fresh insights.

Perhaps your colleague has a brilliant solution for addressing rambunctious behavior or a foolproof plan for an upcoming field trip that doesn't involve a questionable bus driver. Listening to their perspectives and experiences allows you to build a richer foundation for your own decision-making, helping you avoid pioneering choices that leave you feeling more lost than a toddler in a corn maze.

Additionally, remember the power of intuition. There are moments in teaching when you'll face a snap decision that requires no time for discussion or deliberation - think about that awkward silence after a suggestion for a class activity that bombed harder than a lead balloon. In these situations, trusting your gut feeling can be a lifesaver. If your instincts shout, "This class needs to switch gears stat!" you'd do well to heed them. Keeping a clear head in confusing situations allows that inner voice to emerge, guiding your choices even when the stakes feel as high as a senior skipping class during graduation practice.

Ultimately, decision-making under pressure is all about balance. By engaging in reflective practices after high-pressure moments, you'll be better prepared the next time lightning strikes and you need to harness your inner superhero while wearing your trusty "teacher" cape.

In conclusion, the ability to make effective decisions under pressure is an art in itself. By embracing the chaos, trusting your instincts, leveraging experience, seeking collaboration, and channeling your inner Zen master, you can navigate the wild and wondrous world of the classroom. So, the next time you find yourself facing a dilemma, see those moments as opportunities ripe for laughter and reflection - because sometimes, even the most difficult choices lead to surprising moments of creativity and connection! And trust me, laughter is always the best answer in those frantic teaching moments.

PART EIGHT
CLASSROOM MANAGEMENT TECHNIQUES

ESTABLISHING CLASSROOM EXPECTATIONS

Establishing classroom expectations is like laying the groundwork for a solid building: without it, your educational edifice might just crumble at the first sign of turbulence - or, you know, a student sneezing. Just think of it: you walk into class on the first day, and there's a palpable energy buzzing in the air-a mash-up of excitement, anxiety, and that faint smell of a forgotten lunch from last week. It's crucial to put down some ground rules before chaos ensues. As a retired cop, I know a thing or two about rules-mostly the ones broken by surly teenagers pretending to be covert spies as they sneak popcorn during my riveting lecture on what to wear to a job interview.

So, how do you go about establishing these expectations? First, you need a kick-off meeting. Nope, I'm not talking about an all-out brawl for dominance - a simple class meeting will do wonders. Bring everyone together and let's avoid the cliché of "silence is golden" because teenagers could sell sunflowers in a snowstorm if you let them. It's about letting your students speak up! In my experience, the best way to fulfill this requirement is not to bore them to death by reciting rules like an automated traffic camera on repeat. So, I break it down: instead of a lecture, we make a game of it. Students remember the best when they're engaged. And oh boy, do they love a little bit of theatrics!

Next up, practical expectations. Now, I can already hear the collective groan about having to sit up straight and pay attention - what are we, in kindergarten? But dear reader, let me spell it out for you: classroom expectations should be realistic while challenging. Think of fundamental guidelines like "Respect each other" - which, to be clear, does NOT mean "steal someone's pen and claim it's a peace offering." It also includes being on time, which we both know can be a Herculean task for a teenager who suddenly needs to decide if today is a "long hair or short hair" day. Your goal as a teacher is to balance the dread of prison guards with the empathy of a trusted pet owner. It's completely achievable if you know how to sweeten the pot, big time!

Let's not forget about visual reminders! I work in a school where I have to use other classrooms for what I teach (Not enough room I guess to have my own). So, I choose a small section of the white board and write some of the rules that the principal expects to see, not to mention some target academic goals which according to some research, accomplishes nothing. Although, when a group of kids are talking, I stop and point to the learning targets and it immediately brings them back on task and they pay attention! Not sure if you picked up on the sarcasm. Most high school students know what it means to be respectful. I have set expectations long ago with my students therefore they know what to do. If they want me to respect them, then they need to respect me. Now I'd be lying if I said I never called a student's parent in the middle of a class and put them on speaker phone! This usually fixes most behavior problems after the 1st call.

Once we have our core expectations established, a little reinforcement goes a long way. No, I'm not talking about handcuffing the perpetrators when they "forget" the rules.

Now, let's address the elephant in the classroom: once expectations are established, they'll inevitably be tested - just like a science experiment gone wrong, where the proverbial lava erupts, and students scatter like cartoon characters in a dangerous chase scene! When a rule gets bent or broken, discuss it. Keep it light, keep it funny! Use that opportunity to revisit the expectations. "Remember when we discussed respect? Thanks for that demonstration of how NOT to put your phone on vibrate in the middle of my riveting lecture. Let's reformulate those expectations, shall we?"

In summary, establishing classroom expectations is a dynamic and ongoing process. It's a vibrant negotiation where humor must flow, and flexibility is key. You expertly light the path for your future scholars so they can march confidently toward academic achievement. But let's be honest, sometimes these students need a bailiff with a kind heart (that's where I come in). Expectation-setting has the power to shape behavior better than any not-so-cunning plan from a fake spy adventure. And when followed through with consistency, respect, humor, and maybe a little of creativity, it can unlock a treasure chest of potential for the kids who once thought the classroom was a prison of boredom. So, let's embrace the madness and dive into this remarkable, chaotic experience together!

EFFECTIVE COMMUNICATION STRATEGIES

Effective communication strategies in the classroom are like having a Swiss Army knife but made entirely out of patience, humor, and a bit of charisma. If you think about it, communication is the very foundation of our interactions - students who are yelling "POTATO" in the back of class are not doing it to discuss their favorite side dish; they're expressing something! Trust me, as a retired police officer, I've seen all kinds of bizarre communication: the classic "those aren't my drugs" or the eyebrow-raising "But officer, these aren't my pants!" However, in the realm of education, the stakes are higher, and those unforeseen tantrums need to be channeled into constructive dialogue.

First things first, let's talk about body language -yes, that silent yet deafening communicator we often overlook. Having been involved in hundreds of interviews and interrogations, we learn through training to pay attention to body language. Believe it or not, this is something I use every day with my students. Even if I am not teaching and we are merely getting caught up on work, I am constantly observing my students. Hey Michael, is your work that amusing that laughing is helping you answer that algebraic equation? Or is what you're looking at on that phone in your lap causing that smile? Standing in front of a class with knees locked and arms crossed may as well be a neon sign shouting, "I am unapproachable, and I have a hidden stash of lunch detention slips." On the other hand, an open posture with an inviting smile -cue the daylight shining through the classroom window - can literally open communication channels quicker than you can say "mandatory reading list." Get comfortable being an expressive human being in the same way I got comfortable after swapping my police uniform for a comfy yet regrettably "dad-like" sweater. Believe it or not, students will respond better when they feel you're genuinely interested in what they have to say.

Now, let's pivot to the art of asking questions. Open-ended inquiries can transform a mundane lecture into a riveting discussion. Instead of the time worn "Do we understand?" followed by the unsettling silence of crickets chirping, try "What are your thoughts on this topic? And yes, you're allowed to use your phones as calculators, but no TikTok." I do a lot of Socratic Seminars without the paperwork with my students. I will give them a topic or a current event. I ask them what they think. I have found that not long after I ask this question do I already have a debate on my hands. But this teaches critical thinking, communication skills, and how to understand other people's opinions. This slight adjustment invites engagement rather than dismisses it. It encourages students to think critically rather than simply providing you with the winning combo of "A"s on a multiple-choice quiz. Community discourse serves a dual purpose here: it allows everyone to voice their thoughts while inadvertently establishing that you, the educator, have not fully lost your grasp on current slang-bonus points for that!

Of course, and I've already mentioned this, but I cannot forget the importance of active listening. "Yeah, whatever," may be the response you get from a disinterested student, but if you listen intently, it might blossom into something like "Well, I think this topic is important because... "-and there you have it! Understanding students' feelings and perspectives can turn the dullest of subjects into a riveting debate. Listening is not merely a functional skill; it's a superpower! You'll learn about interests, dreams, and even the occasional conspiracy theory involving the cafeteria menu. That's right; listening allows you to become the oracle of the classroom, and who doesn't want to be revered like that?

Now, here comes the sweet spot-feedback. Ah, feedback! It's the magical ingredient that transforms students into budding scholars. However, as with any delicate balance, too much of a good thing can lead to a groaning chorus of "Not the feedback again!" I find it helpful to keep feedback constructive yet humorous. Instead of saying, "Your essay makes about as much sense as a cat wearing a hat," try "Imagining this essay as a delicious tamale, let's just say it could use a better topping." By formatting feedback positively, students are more likely to absorb your critique without sprinting for the door first chance they get.

Having a sense of humor also plays a critical role in building rapport. It assists in diffusing tension and allows for levity in serious discussions. Instead of rigidly lecturing about the repercussions of late assignments, I often take the route of exaggeration: "Late work is like that forgotten round of donuts at a police department meeting: it eventually collects dust and leads to grumpy officers missing out!" Applying humor helps to forge a stronger connection with your students, allowing them to feel safe enough to ask questions and engage more freely with the material.

Remember, effective communication is not just limited to verbal dialogues; written communication, too, has its place. Simple and clear emails can make life easier-don't forget that. With technology at our fingertips, emails will be a huge part of communication once the students graduate. Now don't assume your students know how to send an email. If an expectation is to use email as communication, teach your students how to send an email. How can you set an expectation that they can't accomplish. A gentle reminder of the upcoming test, punctuated by the fact that it's "not going to be as painful as a root canal," goes a long way in achieving success in parent-student interactions.

In conclusion, effective communication strategies are multi-faceted, blending patience with curiosity, and active listening with humor. Students will thrive when they feel understood and approached with warmth. Trust me, the potential for learning skyrockets when you transform your classroom into a space for open dialogue, where every "POTATO" comment is a valid contribution. So, let's strap on our metaphorical helmets, break down those walls, and embark on the wonderfully unpredictable journey of fostering effective communication; one unexpected potato comment at a time!

ENGAGEMENT TECHNIQUES FOR ALL LEARNING STYLES

Engagement techniques for all learning styles are a crucial component of the modern classroom, which can feel like trying to nail Jell-o to a wall -challenging yet oddly satisfying when executed correctly. Every student comes with a unique assortment of learning preferences. You've got your visual learners, your auditory types, the kinesthetic folks who must get up and dance their way through lessons, and everyone in between. As a retired cop, blending these techniques feels like building a case - one where every bit of evidence adds to the grand strategy of keeping my classroom stimulating.

First and foremost, let's chat about the visual learners. If you've ever watched a kid's eyes glaze over amid a monologue about the Pythagorean theorem, it's time to level up your game! For these savvy learners, incorporating colorful diagrams, info-graphics, and videos can help to bring the lesson to life. Now, I know what you might be thinking: "Josh, can't I just put up a screen and call it a day?" Well, yes and no! Think beyond the typical PowerPoint presentation filled with unreadable text larger than the Hall of Justice. Instead, use visuals that tell a story -a comic strip illustrating math concepts can make a potentially dull lesson into a visual epic. Trust me; it's like turning plain cereal into a gourmet breakfast.

Then there are the auditory learners, those multi-tasking maestros who could probably listen to a lecture while skateboarding down a hill. For them, discussions, debates, and interactive lectures are of utmost importance. Techniques like "turn and talk" give students the chance to discuss a topic with a partner rather than listening to me drone on like a fly buzzing in the classroom. For added flair, I often utilize music to reinforce ideas; no, I'm not suggesting a disco party, but a carefully curated playlist of thematic music might just do the trick. Catchy tunes help reinforce concepts, and who knows, a Bee Gees song about multiplication tables might just be the breakthrough we've all been waiting for! When I was teaching middle school special education in North Carolina, I wrote a song about triangles and played it on the guitar. That was 20 years ago and I'm not that creative now, but if you are musically inclined, maybe it'll work for you.

Next up are the kinesthetic learners - those champions of action. If you've got a student with the wiggly legs, the fidget spinner in one hand, and a propensity to lean out of their chair like a sailor on the Titanic, you've encountered a kinesthetic learner in their natural habitat. These students thrive on hands-on experiences -the kind were sitting still for extended periods could induce a spontaneous eruption resembling those classic volcano science experiments. Here's where the real fun happens bring in activities! Group projects involving building a model or a creative role-playing scenario can hit the sweet spot for these students. I do a lot of life skills in my classes. I teach things such as cooking, careers, how to use jumper cables, how to tie a tie for an interview, and how to change a tire. I even taught "what to do when you are pulled over by the police". I got with the school resource officer, and we set up real scenarios. Not only did they receive instruction that is sure to help them at some point, but it helped the students become more comfortable around the offi- cer. Need to practice history? Why not have them reenact a pivotal event? It's a recipe for chaos, but also a sure-fire way to engage them fully. The laughter shared during a mock battle can turn facts into treasured memories, rather than crumpled pages tossed into the trash.

Now, let's not forget our introverted learners, who may not be as vocal in group discussions. These kids often possess thoughts as profound as the universe itself but prefer a quieter place to express them. This is where journaling and online discussions come in handy. Allowing your students the freedom to reflect in writing or post to a learning management system fosters a sense of agency. Their ideas become vibrant threads woven into the classroom tapestry -without the fear of public speaking turning them into a deer caught in headlights.

Incorporating technology is another magical ingredient in engaging all students. Interactive educational apps and gamified learning platforms can turn a history lesson into a virtual escape room or a math problem into a fast-paced digital game. Picture a scenario where your class explores ancient civilizations while immersed in a fantasy video game! The possibilities are nearly endless when technology meets creativity. Plus, let's be honest, anything that gives me a break from my endless lecture is a win in my book.

Finally, it's vital to build a classroom culture where students feel comfortable learning in their own styles. Creating a supportive atmosphere where students are encouraged to explore various approaches fosters confidence. This is essential for allowing students to put their own flair into lessons. Whether it's an impromptu debate on the merits of pineapple on pizza or a group project on ecosystems that integrates models built from recycled materials, embracing creativity can turn engagement techniques into an absolute triumph.

Engagement techniques for all learning styles are truly about blending the right mix of tactics -think of it as a magic potion tailored to the unique personalities in your classroom. When you incorporate vibrant visuals for the visual learners, energetic discussions for the auditory types, hands-on activities for the kinesthetic kids, and supportive environments for the more timid souls, what you'll witness is the transformation of learning into a delightful adventure! May the classroom chaos reign, but within that chaos, let's shine a light of engaging discovery. Now that's a recipe for success!

MANAGING DISRUPTIVE BEHAVIOR

Managing disruptive behavior in the classroom can feel like herding cats-well, pyrotechnic cats on caffeine. Trust me, I know a thing or two about disruption. I spent years on the streets as a police officer dealing with unruly suspects. But now, I find myself face-to-face with a different type of chaos: students tossing around paper airplanes and food instead of bags of illegal substances. It's a slippery slope, but what's crucial is how we, as educators, navigate that slope without tumbling down into a bottomless pit of madness-or worse, a deluge of crumpled worksheets.

First, let's establish a basic principle: disruptive behavior often stems from the desire for attention. Think about it: if a student pops up with a question that's completely off topic - "Hey, Mr. U, can we bring pet iguanas to class?" -they're likely just seeking to break the monotony of traditional learning. It's our job to recognize this developmental quirk and, rather than extinguishing their fire, channel that energy into something productive. Instead of the dreaded glare of disapproval (you know, the one that could shame a raccoon rummaging through the garbage), swap it out for a little humor! A quick, "I'm all for exotic animals, but let's save iguanas for show-and-tell day!" can diffuse the situation.

Next up, we have the golden rule of "know thy enemy" -aka understanding the reasons behind the disruptive behavior. Each interruption is a clue, perhaps a breadcrumb trail leading to deeper issues. Is the student constantly chatting with their buddy because they're bored or maybe struggling with the material? Channel your inner detective: observe the dynamics in the classroom more closely. Like a cop on a stakeout, keep an eye on those secret whispers, the fidgeting hands, and the strategic glances they share. Once you decode their intentions, you can proactively address their needs by adapting your teaching methods or activities. Maybe a hands-on group project would be the antidote to their boredom -anything to keep them invested without resorting to the old reliable text venturing into battlefield territory!

Now let's talk about pre-emptive actions. I wouldn't walk into a warrant gone wrong without proper backup and I certainly wouldn't start a lesson without ground rules and routines in place. By implementing clear expectations from day one, you equip yourself with a strong foundation - of "disruption armor." Students know the rules, and you reinforce them through laughter, games, and positive reinforcement! A simple "If we can keep the paper airplanes in the 'no-fly zone' today, every student will earn a point toward our class party!" This can turn a cheeky disruption into a cooperative pursuit.

However, even with the best-laid plans, the unpredictable still occurs. Enter the legendary "restorative conversation" -a fantastical dialogue aimed at resolving the hiccup at hand. When a student makes a ruckus during quiet missing work time (cue the dramatic sigh), it's vital to address it promptly. But wait! Don't spring into action with a "Who do you think you are?" approach. Instead, opt for a more civilized interrogation, "What led you to think that enchanting melodies of chupacabra videos were more enticing than the fine literary work we're diving into today?" This acknowledges their behavior while making it clear that an alternative approach is reading the room instead. These conversations are about understanding, accountability, and finding solutions - miniature negotiations akin to getting pesky neighborhood kids to return stolen lawn gnomes.

As you embark down the path of addressing disruptive behavior, believe it or not, a large part of the solution requires reinforcing positive behavior instead of solely punishing the negative. Create an ecosystem where good behavior is celebrated like the rare diamond it is. A simple shout-out, points for proper participation, or a surprise lunch with the teacher can go a long way. By creating conditions that reward desirable actions, students will prioritize engagement over disruption -and let's face it, who doesn't like a high-five and a few accolades?

Lastly, one of the most crucial aspects is to manage the delicate fusion of empathy and authority. Yes, you want to establish order, but you also want students to feel safe. They should appreciate the importance of respect while becoming aware of their impact on others. Effective yet empathetic interventions allow students to become aware of their actions and the ripple effect they may cause. "Hey, buddy, I know you're passionate about your iguana idea, but we're reading right now. Let's save that for later so everyone can enjoy the stories!" It's all about striking that perfect balance between being 'the teacher' and 'the cool teacher who gets it.'

So here we are, navigating the murky waters of managing disruptive behavior! By understanding the motives behind the actions, preemptively establishing clear expectations, reinforcing positive choices, and engaging in meaningful conversations, we've created a strategic plan for success. Classroom disruption may never entirely vanish all together. Kids are kids-but with the right mindset (and maybe an emergency stash of snacks, we can transform chaos into a thriving learning environment. Now, who wants an iguana for show-and-tell? Just kidding!

EVALUATING AND ADJUSTING MANAGEMENT TECHNIQUES

Evaluating and adjusting management techniques in the classroom is akin to carefully tuning a sports car - you've got to know how to delicately tweak the brakes while making sure the engine is humming beautifully. As a retired police officer, I know all about finding that sweet spot in high-tempo environments. Just when you think you've mastered the art of teaching, students come in with fresh faces and fresh chaos, and you realize your finely tuned machine is more "clunker" than a "1975 Ford Bronco." But fear not, my fellow educators; it's all part of the wild ride.

First things first: self-reflection is an absolute must when you're evaluating management techniques. It's time to don your metaphorical monocle, take a step back, and assess what's been working and what's taken a nosedive faster than a failing reality TV show. Ask yourself whether the techniques you're using are resonating with the students or simply causing an eye roll that could knock a football player sideways. Did you try a new behavior chart that was supposed to sparkle and shine like a diamond but ended up looking like crumpled aluminum foil? Reflecting on your practices allows you to identify successes, as well as flops, without getting too emotionally attached as if they were your beloved pet hamster.

Next is the power of data, yes, I said it! Data might not sound as exciting as diving into the latest trends on social media, but when it comes to evaluating management techniques, it's invaluable. Whether it's tracking attendance, behavior incidents, or even those coveted grades, numbers paint a clear picture of what's happening in your classroom. Think of yourself as a detective gathering evidence -only instead of chasing crooks, you're chasing insights. I've found that keeping an eye on trends can unveil behaviors we might have missed. Maybe you realize that Mondays are bigger circus acts than a polka-dotted tent at a county fair. Knowing when your students are at their most rambunctious (Hello, Monday morning!) can help you strategize and then hit them with a fun and engaging lesson before the weekend feels all too distant!

In addition to data, seek input from your students. The geniuses who reside in your classroom are often the best sources of information on how things are really running, sometimes with the brutal honesty of a toddler critiquing a painting. Utilize anonymous surveys or engage them in casual discussions about what's working and what feels about as appealing as soggy cereal. "How are we feeling about our group activities? Do they excite you? Or do you dream of climbing Mount Everest instead?" Receiving feedback fosters a sense of inclusion and shows your students their voices matter, and who knows, you might find that they crave more of that engaging hands-on learning instead of the monotony of standard lectures.

After gathering data and insights, it's time to implement changes. Adjusting management techniques doesn't mean throwing the baby out with the bathwater; rather, you're refining what you've already implemented. Start small; perhaps tweak the seating arrangements to find the right chemistry. You might find that grouping certain personalities together sparks creativity, while separating your class clown from the architect of chaos is a recipe for better behavior. Sometimes, students need a bit of a shake-up to reignite their interest, and subtle shifts can lead to gradual improvement!

Now for the real magic! Paying attention to the effectiveness of the adjustments is crucial. Have those management changes yielded results? Monitor your classroom atmosphere and behaviors. Is there more participation, fewer distractions, and fewer attempts to plant a remote-controlled fart box in each other's backpacks? The changes are working! In this stage, remember the importance of adaptability. Just like a chameleon changes color, be prepared to adapt when things aren't going as expected. If you find yourself observing a spike in distractions following a new rule or activity, it's time to rethink and adjust your approach accordingly, rather than stubbornly plowing through with a set plan.

By maintaining a lighthearted approach, classroom management can feel overwhelming, like trying to juggle chainsaws at times. When students engage in less-than-ideal behaviors, use humor to diffuse the situation rather than frustration. "I thought I signed up to teach! Not for a color war between paper airplanes!" Lightheartedness will not only keep the learning environment manageable but also create a positive atmosphere where students feel valued and excited to participate in the conversation.

In summary, evaluating and adjusting management techniques is a dynamic process, one that requires both reflection and adaptability. By embracing feedback from your data, students, and observations while maintaining an open mind and a dose of humor, you can create a thriving classroom environment. Remember, the ride may be zany, unpredictable, and at times chaotic, but you're not in it alone. Grab the wheel, savor the adventure, and keep steering your classroom toward the most exhilarating destination: productive learning that maintains a little pizazz!

PART NINE
THE ROLE OF EMPATHY IN TEACHING

THE VALUE OF EMPATHY IN EDUCATION

As a retired cop, I never dreamed I'd be dishing out daily doses of empathy instead of arriving on a crash scene from a high-speed chase. Imagine my surprise when I realized that navigating the hallways of a high school required more finesse and compassion than wrestling a kid in a too-tight hoodie trying to make a getaway from the lunchroom without paying. Yup, empathy is that secret weapon every teacher neds and let me tell you, it's not just a fancy buzzword thrown around at coffee breaks and professional developments. It's the glue that holds the vast and chaotic universe of high school together - that and duct tape, of course.

Now, let's tackle the pressing question: Why does empathy matter in education? Think of it this way: Imagine walking into a room filled with awkward teenagers sporting varying degrees of angst, confusion, and a smattering of teenage rebellion. If I approached them with the authority of a baton-wielding police officer, how effective do you think my teaching would be?

Spoiler alert: about as effective as teaching a goldfish how to ride a bicycle! But when I inject a little empathy into the mix, magic happens. Suddenly, I'm not just "Mr. U" the teacher -I'm "Mr. U" the relatable human being who gets it.

Empathy in education allows us to connect with our students on a level that goes beyond the sterile classroom environment filled with textbooks and the odor of overcooked pizza on Fridays. It opens the door for genuine relationships where students feel safe to express their feelings, share their concerns, and even admit they forgot to do their homework because they were up playing Fortnite and didn't get any sleep. This connection cultivates a sense of belonging, crucial in a world where many teens feel like they are floating in space without a tether to ground them.

In the heat of the academic combat zone - often referred to as the classroom - emotions can run high. One minute, a student is doodling in their notebook, and the next, they're on the verge of a meltdown because he can't find the NBA card they brought to school that is worth $400. By embracing a sense of empathy, we can recognize when they are struggling emotionally, even if their facial expression is more perplexing than a monkey who's trained to work a video camera. Acknowledging their feelings doesn't mean we indulge in a full-blown therapy session - unless, of course, you're ready to hand out free ice cream to the whole class! It means providing them a moment to pause, breathe, and reset, allowing them to return to their work with a sense of dignity intact rather than feeling like they just bombed a pop quiz.

Moreover, empathy can transform the classroom dynamic. Instead of students feeling like they're in a 'Greatest Hits of Discipline' album, they begin to see the classroom as a sanctuary of support. They're inspired to engage and not because of fear of detention or my ever-watchful eye, but because they genuinely want to participate. When students feel understood by their teachers, they are much more likely to return that understanding, creating a symbiotic relationship that resembles an intricately choreographed dance routine - albeit one that occasionally ends in chaotic hilarity when someone accidentally steps on someone else's foot during a group project.

Now let's not forget the pivotal role empathy plays in academic performance. Research shows that when students feel emotionally supported, they tend to achieve better results! Yes, you heard that right providing a safe space brimming with empathy could be the difference between a student mindfully taking a test or a student who answers C for every question. Who knew that nurturing emotions could do wonders for grades? It's practically groundbreaking!

Ultimately, the value of empathy in education is the secret sauce to our teaching endeavors. It sets the stage for engaged, motivated, and connected students who not only learn but thrive. Isn't that the goal? To turn restless teenagers into confident learners who can tackle the world preferably without the need for handcuffs? So, here's my call to action let's use empathy like confetti in the classrooms and create a positive learning environment that celebrates both academic successes and the beautiful messiness of being human. Now, if only we could get the cafeteria to stop serving mysterious meat on Mondays, we might just hit the jackpot in the education game.

RECOGNIZING EMOTIONAL CUES IN STUDENTS

In my journey as a retired cop, I've learned that recognizing emotional cues in students is akin to being a detective - but instead of interrogating suspects, I'm deciphering the intricacies of teenage angst. Trust me, the stakes are just as high! If I miss the signs, my students could go from quietly doodling in their notebooks to thinking they're starring in a one-act play called "The Emotional Catastrophe." So, how does one become an emotional cue connoisseur? Buckle up, folks; it's a wild ride!

First things first: teenagers are like onions. They have layers, and if you're not careful, you may end up crying like you just sat down with your cat and watched a ASPCA Sarah McLachlan commercial reminding your cat of how good he has it. You might spot a student sitting silently in the back row, staring at the wall as if he's about to confess some deep-seated secret. That's your cue, my friend! Instead of assuming they're simply pondering the meaning of life (or why the cafeteria serves tuna salad in what appears to be the middle of a food apocalypse), it's time to dig deeper. The glazed-over eyes and slumped shoulders can be indicators that something is bubbling under the surface.

Then there's the classic "distraction defense." Every educator knows it well: a student who can't keep their focus on anything other than that mysterious ball of lint rolling across the floor or the ceiling tile that has a suspicious resemblance to the face of Chewbacca. Sure, it's easy to assume this kid just has the attention span of a goldfish. But before you pull out the "Get Off Your Phone!" battle cry, remember -this could be their way of self-soothing during a moment of distress. Recognizing these emotional cues requires us to be a blend of Sherlock Holmes and a concerned family pet -curious yet compassionate.

Let's also explore the phenomenon of sudden verbosity. One minute, a meek student is scribbling on their paper like a deer caught in headlights; the next, they're passionately arguing why they have to dress out for gym. Such wild and passionate outbursts may be based on the emotional landscape they're navigating. Keeping an eye on the rising tide of their expressiveness may give you insight into what's going on inside their heads. If they've morphed from a quiet wallflower to a stand-up comedian, it could spell excitement, confidence, or a desperate cry for help.

Another glaring indicator is the classic "social withdrawal." No, this isn't just them being introverted; it's when a once-active student suddenly goes MIA from group projects and lunch table discussions - leaving their friends wondering if they've turned invisible. If a student who used to enjoy collaborating now huddles in a comer like a wintry woodland creature, it might be worth investigating. Understanding emotional cues means paying attention to the shifts in their social behavior. After all, this isn't just a wild costume party where everyone can disappear and reappear at will; it could signify a struggle that needs addressing.

Now, of course, we must touch upon the star players of emotional expression: facial expressions and body language. Think of it as your personal emotional radar. Students can communicate a wealth of info with just a quirked eyebrow, a nervous foot tap, or a mysterious frown that looks suspiciously like they've just tasted an awful almond-flavored essence in their snacks. As an educator, tuning into these non-verbal signals becomes our superpower, allowing us to address concerns before they spiral into chaos worthy of a soap opera.

Understanding these emotional cues isn't about playing amateur therapist, because, let's be honest, none of us want to be stuck navigating the emotionally complicated lives of teenagers like we're caught in a poorly scripted drama. It's simply about establishing a connection where students feel comfortable sharing their experiences. By cultivating an environment that encourages honest discussions about feelings, we can help our students understand that it's totally okay to bring their emotions to class, as long as they keep themselves in check.

So, there you have it, the art of recognizing emotional cues in students, presented with the delightful chaos that is adolescence in mind. It's about transforming ourselves into filter detectors of feeling, aware of the subtle signs that reveal what's happening under the surface. Pay attention to those emotional cues, and who knows? You might just save the day - or at the very least, prevent a dramatic outburst involving pencil sharpeners, lunch trays, or a rogue slice of cafeteria pizza launching into orbit. Empathy and insight, my friends-it's the secret ingredient in the recipe for a successful classroom experience!

BUILDING CONNECTIONS THROUGH SHARED EXPERIENCES

As I stood in front of my classroom, armed with a dry-erase marker and an inexplicable longing for the days when absolute silence was an option in a police interrogation room, I realized the importance of shared experiences. It's like the secret sauce of education-when teachers and students' bond over moments that go beyond textbooks. These connections create an environment where students flourish and actually want to learn, instead of treating education like a trip to the dentist, filled with anxiety and a desperate longing for candy afterward.

Now, let's be real: teenagers can be some of the most perplexing creatures on the planet. They oscillate between drama queens, philosophers, and giggling hyenas at the drop of a hat. But what they all have in common is their profound need for connection. When I first made the transition from police work to teaching, I expected to be met with a wall of indifference. Instead, I discovered that by sharing experiences, whether that was celebrating a small victory or commiserating over lost homework, I could cut through that wall quicker than a butter knife through a warm stick of margarine.

One of my favorite tactics has been storytelling. Let me clarify: I'm not suggesting I stand before my class like a sad, aging bard trying to get a group of disinterested teens to pay attention. No, my stories are peppered with absurdity, colorful characters (who may or may not be based on students), and plenty of humor. I love to share the awkward moments from my law enforcement days - like the time I accidentally dropped a motorist's driver's license in between the seat and the middle console. How can you not connect over the mutual embarrassment of being human? Those anecdotes draw laughter, build trust, and create a bridge where they feel comfortable sharing their own stories.

In the same vein, I've learned that experiencing things together - in and out of the classroom - can work wonders for engagement. When kids witness their peers' questionable yet hilarious attempts at a three-legged race, it generates an unspoken bond, stemming from those collective giggles and shared moments of mutual embarrassment. And let's not forget that everyone leaves a reason to point and laugh at each other, right? The undoubtedly awkward moments-accidentally kneeing your best friend in the shin while trying to spin them in a Game. This creates friendships that are solidified through laughter, and wham! Instant connections are formed!

And let's not ignore the role of music. Ah, sweet, sweet music - the great uniter of teenagers, who often tend to use their earbuds to drown out the world. Integrating music into my lessons has sparked unexpected dialogues about creativity, emotion, and culture. During study skills lessons, I might throw on a groovy tune or two to illustrate a decade. There's nothing quite as satisfying as watching students bob their heads to the grunge era music scene while connecting historical events to the beats they can relate to. We may even engage in a spontaneous dance-off during a "brain break." It's hard to deny that busting out your best moves (even if they are completely terrible) alongside your teacher adds a dash of authenticity to our bond, and trust me, you'll never again hear the end of it when a student catches me attempting the "moonwalk."

Ultimately, building connections through shared experiences transforms the classroom from a static environment into a vibrant community of understanding, support, and laughter. It's about connecting with each student on a personal level, fostering an atmosphere where they feel valued and recognized - not just as numbers in a system. Watching a group of seemingly disinterested teenagers morph into a supportive circle as they relate to one another is truly gratifying. In the end, it's not about making a perfect score on a test; it's about teaching my students that they matter, their voices matter, and that laughter can transcend all boundaries, allowing us to sing, dance, and embrace the fabulous messiness that is high school. So remember, in the game of education, shared experiences are what keep us all in it for the laughs, the chaos, and the inevitable bonding moments we'll look back on fondly - and, most importantly, the creation of memories we can all cherish for the rest of our lives!

PART TEN
THE WEIGHT OF EXPECTATIONS

UNDERSTANDING THE WEIGHT OF ACADEMIC EXPECTATIONS

As a retired cop turned special education teacher, I've often found myself in the oddest of situations. I've dealt with everything from unruly civilians and students, to unexpected school lockdowns involving a swatting call. However, nothing haunts the hallways of high schools quite like the specter of academic expectations. Picture this: you've got a group of teenagers, hormone levels off the hook, violations of the dress code, and my Jordan's are better than yours also juggling the pressure of tests, homework, and that little voice in their heads screaming: "You have to graduate!" Welcome to the high school pressure cooker.

Academic pressure affects all students even if they don't admit it and it weighs heavier on students than the backpack of books they lug around daily. Face it, in this day and age, a D on a report card can either make a student feel like they've committed a federal offense or like they passed and that's all that matters. And let's not even talk about the "parental expectations" lurking just outside the classroom like a pack of wolves waiting for a moment of weakness. These kids are not just contending with their own aspirations; they are effectively classroom warriors, fighting on two fronts-the battlefield of academics and the minefield of parental approval.

But here's the kicker: these expectations can often become a double-edged sword. On one side, they serve as a driving force, pushing students to achieve their potential, but on the flip side, they can create an ecosystem of fear, anxiety, and despair. From my time in law enforcement, I learned how easily pressure can lead individuals to act irrationally. Teenagers experience anxiety at levels that would send even the toughest cop to a stress ball factory; the kinds of stress that lead to the famous "senioritis" or the all too familiar "why bother?" syndrome. It's like trying to teach a goat to climb a tree: entirely possible, but it's going to be an uphill struggle, literally.

So, how do we combat this suffocating atmosphere of expectations? For starters, we need to establish a solid foundation of understanding within the classroom. As teachers, we must recognize that every student is wrestling with their own demons, whether it's the fear of not being good enough to make the varsity team or worrying that their grades will send their parents into a fit. Communicating with students about these feelings, validating their experiences, and letting them know they aren't alone can make all the difference. I often say, "Hey, it's okay to make mistakes and not pass! "It took me 3 tries before I passed my driver's test too"!

Another important consideration is to help students develop realistic and achievable goals. Let's be honest: not everyone is destined to be the next Einstein or Beyoncé. And that's fine! Recognizing strengths and passions-whether they lie in art, theater, or even being the reigning champion of the cafeteria's "Who can balance the most food on their head?" contest-is crucial. Encouraging students to focus on their unique gifts can ease some of that suffocating weight of expectations. After all, academic excellence isn't just about getting perfect scores; it's about preparing for life outside of high school where, let's face it, no one is going to ask for your GPA at a job interview.

Admittedly, we should also be forthright about the consequences of neglecting education, but with a dose of humor. When I tell my students, "You can't expect to survive on ramen noodles and TikTok fame," I can almost hear the collective eye rolls, but they get the point. Humor can be a great equalizer, allowing students to view academic expectations in less terrifying terms.

Finally, let's remember that while we want students to excel, we also have to remind them that life is rife with ups and downs. They will face failure, just like how I face a gym bench press whenever I haven't lifted weights in months. The key takeaway here is that we need to create a culture that celebrates improvement, hard work, and resilience over mere outcomes. After all, if you can dodge a wrench, you can dodge a D-and trust me, both have a tendency to come flying your way when you least expect it!

Navigating the weight of academic expectations is no easy task, but with humor, understanding, and the right support, we can help our students learn to lift that weight and maybe, just maybe, even put up a max weight.

RECOGNIZING THE EMOTIONAL NEEDS OF STUDENTS

The emotional needs of students - those mysterious beasts shadowing every classroom, lurking beneath the surface, and often resulting in more drama than a daytime soap opera. As a special education teacher, I've come to learn that those teenage years are a rollercoaster of emotions, and they're riding it without a seatbelt. One minute a student is happy as a clam, and the next, they resemble a hulking ball of stress and anxiety the size of an angry bear. It can be bewildering - at times, downright comical if you have the right lens. One moment they're singing Ice Cube at the top of their lungs, and the next, they're sulking in the comer like they just lost a game of dodgeball in gym class.

To say that adolescents face a plethora of emotional challenges is an understatement. From peer relationships to academic pressures, their emotional needs can rival the complexity of a rubix cube. And here we are, the educators, armed with nothing but a whiteboard marker and a questionable supply of granola bars, trying to navigate this maze of feelings. It's like being a traffic cop in a parking lot during Black Friday. You've got to keep everything running smoothly, yet no one seems to pay attention to your signals-or worse, they treat those signals like they're nothing more than suggestions, leading them into emotional pileups that make your head spin.

It's also essential to create an atmosphere where emotions can be expressed without fear of judgment. You've got to encourage an open dialogue about feelings, like a friendly chat between buddies at the gym, except minus the sweaty headlocks. Let's face it, when teens feel comfortable to voice their fears, frustrations, or joy, it's like the weights been lifted off their shoulders. They shouldn't feel like they need to wear a mask of indifference; we need to let them know that it's more than okay to let their guard down, even if that means sharing about their disastrous first date or last weekend's epic TikTok fail.

Managing students' emotional well-being often comes with its own set of challenges, akin to trying to contain a herd of bouncing kangaroos. Some may act out internally, leading to behavioral problems in the classroom, while others might do an about-face ino cheerful irreverence as a coping mechanism. It's essential for us to recognize that it's all connected - what happens outside the classroom can deeply affect what transpires within those four walls. When I taught emotional and behavior support in downtown Pittsburgh, I had a class of 12 students. All of these students came from some really bad areas of the city. Every Monday morning, I had to have a half hour conversation allowing them to vent about all the things they had to deal with over the weekend. Most of my students witnessed domestic violence, drive by shootings, dead bodies, and drug deals. If I did not give them the opportunity to vent on Monday mornings, my entire week was a disaster. The academic setting must be a sanctuary, a gym for mental resilience as much as it is for cramming for exams.

In understanding their emotional needs, we also have to shine a light on the necessity of coping strategies. High school isn't just an academic training ground; it is a crash course in life! Teaching students how to manage stress is a real-life skill. I'm certainly not saying that I have all the answers (I still pull out my hair trying to remember where I put my keys half the time), but I do know this: Providing support through education leads to personal growth, and reminding our students that it's okay to stumble on the road to self-discovery is essential.

Recognizing the emotional needs of our students may feel like a daunting task. When we can create an environment where students feel safe expressing their feelings, then that's half the battle. In the end, it's less about being their therapist and more about being that supportive figure they can count on, just as they'd rely on a buddy to spot them during a squat. After all, we're in this together, so let's lift each other up!

THE ROLE OF TEACHERS IN SUPPORTING STUDENT WELL-BEING

The noble role of the teacher - guardian of knowledge, cultivator of curiosity, and sometimes, whether they like it or not, an impromptu therapist. As a retired police officer, I have seen my share of wild things, but nothing prepares you for the emotional rollercoaster that is high school. In this day and age, teachers play an absolutely pivotal role in supporting student well-being and navigating that position is essential.

To make a real impact, teachers must create a classroom environment that resembles less of a military obstacle course and more of a safe haven where students feel comfortable to explore their feelings. That means ditching the "no talking during class" rule and embracing an open dialogue that encourages students to share their thoughts and emotions - even if sometimes those thoughts involve the juicy details of the latest school drama. By fostering a space where laughter and transparency are welcome, teachers can break clown the walls of anxiety that can at times feel like a gargantuan fortress. And yes, we all know that inner fortress can be fortified by defensiveness and awkward high school social dynamics - the kind where everyone is plotting the downfall of their arch-nemesis without ever really speaking up.

Furthermore, teachers must keep their own mental health in check. After all, you can't pour from an empty cup, and you definitely can't lead a high school war against anxiety while feeling like you've just been steamrolled by a runaway school bus. This means prioritizing self-care and modeling positive coping strategies for students. Whether we set aside time for meditation, belong to a book club, or engage in a serious love affair with weightlifting (which, full disclosure, I've been guilty of), we set a powerful precedent that prioritizing one's mental health leads to a healthier, happier life.

In short, the role of teachers in supporting student well-being is integral, akin to the cheese on a pizza - without it, things can get pretty bland. We need to create an atmosphere of empathy and connection, nurture emotional intelligence, and remind students - through action and humor-that it's perfectly acceptable to stumble along the way. So, let's arm ourselves with patience, humor, and the occasional reward of pizza parties for all! Together, we can navigate the often-chaotic sea of teenage emotions and emerge on the other side shouting "I survived!" In this wild ride of teaching, our genuine support can truly help students flourish and thrive. Here's to being the wacky, wise, and wonderful guides they need!

PROMOTING HEALTHY COPING MECHANISMS FOR STUDENTS

Promoting healthy coping mechanisms for students is like teaching them to ride a bike: a bit wobbly at first, but with practice and perseverance, they'll eventually zoom off into the sunset, pedals flying and hair blowing in the wind. As a special ed teacher, I can confidently say that navigating the choppy waters of adolescence is no easy feat. Students often experience stressors that can feel daunting, from homework overload to social media drama that can escalate quicker than a high-speed chase. So, it's our job to arm them with the tools they need to handle life's curveballs without losing their marbles - and without dodging basketballs in gym class.

First and foremost, we have to normalize the conversation around stress and anxiety. Too many students feel like they're stuck in a one-person soliloquy while their classmates are starring in a comedy ensemble. When teachers openly discuss stress - whether it's brought on by a tough math test or a looming prom date - their walls come down faster than a door being hit with a ram serving a search warrant.

This lighter approach can make students feel more comfortable about expressing their own challenges and relying on healthier strategies to cope, instead of resorting to Fit of Rage #837 in the cafeteria over a misplaced binder.

Next up is introducing students to the wondrous world of stress-relief techniques. Breathing exercises, mindfulness, and physical activities are like the holy trinity of healthy coping mechanisms. Teach them simply to breathe. Trust me, when the pressure ramps up and they feel like they're trying to breathe underwater, the last thing they want to think about is "correct breathing techniques." A simple exercise counting to four as they inhale, holding for four, and exhaling for four -can help reduce anxiety levels. Encouraging students to try yoga or guided meditation is like offering them a magic shield to ward off the dragons of stress. They might scoff at first, but when they discover how surprisingly relaxing it can be, you'll have them chanting "om" at every turn.

Art, music, and drama encourage self-expression in ways that help students unload their burdens. I often tell students that if they make a mess while creating, it's just part of the artistic process. Chaos can be a catalyst for creativity much like how my morning coffee often morphs into a "how many times am I going to misplace my keys"! Perhaps suggest that they keep a journal or sketch their feelings and thoughts, allowing them to transform anger into art. It can serve as a healthy distraction from whatever cosmic storm is brewing in their minds.

Another powerful coping strategy involves regular exercise. It's like science fiction but grounded in reality: physical activity releases endorphins, those magical little neurotransmitters that help fight stress and lift spirits. Students don't need to become gym rats overnight; simply walking, dancing, or joining a sports team can work wonders. As a weightlifting enthusiast (I can bench press my own expectations!), I emphasize the need for students to find activities they enjoy.

Don't underestimate the golden perks of stretching! A simple stretch can unleash tension that has been plaguing the student since the weekend.

Let's also address the importance of peer support. Encouraging students to lean on friends during tough times is crucial. Their clique can be like a pit crew ready to patch up and recharge their emotional tires when they hit a bump in the road. Promote healthy interactions and friendship-building activities and watch friendships blossom - it's like planting a garden where all the personalities are blooming like colorful flowers. We all know that sometimes laughter can come from the most unexpected places, and having a supportive crew during stressful times makes life's challenges feel a lot more manageable.

Promoting healthy coping mechanisms isn't a one-and-done scenario but a journey composed of various tools that students can draw upon as they navigate both high school and life after graduation. It's about providing them with options and encouraging them to experiment with different strategies until they find what works best. So, let's empower our students to embrace their challenges, laugh through the struggles, and roll through the ups and downs like the brave emotional warriors they are. After all, high school is but a chapter in their story, and with the right coping mechanisms, they can turn the pages confidently!

PART ELEVEN
ENGAGING STUDENTS THROUGH FITNESS

THE BENEFITS OF PHYSICAL ACTIVITY IN EDUCATION

As a retired police officer turned special education teacher, I've seen my fair share of quirky situations. But let me tell you, nothing is quirkier than trying to wrangle a room full of teenagers who haven't moved an inch since the last bell. It's like trying to herd chickens. Physical activity doesn't just keep them from becoming chair-shaped, though. Nope! It has a ton of benefits that reach far beyond the gym or the weight room. First off, let's address the elephant in the room - or should I say, the marshmallow! Mental health among our kids is at an all-time high in terms of need, there is nothing better than a solid sweat session to lift those spirits. When kids break a sweat, they're releasing endorphins, those magical little hormones that make them feel all warm and fuzzy inside. Have you ever seen a teenager come into class after running a mile? They're basically glowing! I like to imagine the light coming off of them is like their own personal "I just exercised!" spotlight. They're not just walking into the classroom; they're strutting in like they've just won the lottery-unfortunately, without the actual lottery winnings.

And as much as we'd love to believe that a student can power through an entire day of math, science, and English without any movement, that thought is about as fictional as a unicorn riding a skateboard. Studies have shown that when students are physically active, their brains become sharper. This is crucial when you're trying to decipher whether that snapchat video looped ten times in a row is educational or just endless teenage antics. I taught a class right after gym/weight training. The students who had the gym class were much more attentive and participated more than they did during the first period. There was definitely a difference between the students coming from gym and the ones who didn't have gym. More oxygen and energy mean more focus on their studies, which is music to my ears as a teacher. If we can get them moving even a little, we might just have their undivided attention - at least until the next group chat explodes!

Physical activity also fosters teamwork and cooperation among students. After all, nothing brings a group together quite like the struggle to complete a relay race while avoiding tripping over each other's sneakers. When students engage in physical activities like team sports or group exercises, they learn crucial skills such as communication, strategy, and respect for one another's competitive prowess-or lack thereof. Plus, seeing your fellow student roll their ankle trying to dunk a basketball can build camaraderie that no textbook can replicate. If they can survive that painful moment together, they can likely tackle any academic challenge life throws their way!

Now, let's not forget the lifelong benefits of incorporating fitness into the education system. We're not just talking about getting these kids through high school; we want to equip them with skills that last well beyond those dreaded exams. Learning how to enjoy physical activity early on can instill habits that create a healthier lifestyle as adults. As a former cop, I can assure you that maintaining your health is key if you ever want to do something as mundane as chasing down a suspect or, more importantly, keeping up with your kids during family outings! Trust me, you do not want to be that parent panting on the sidelines asking for a bench to sit on while your toddler races off chasing fireflies.

Let's consider all the fun ways to get kids moving. Have you ever seen someone attempt to learn the dance moves on the video game "Just Dance?" It's hilarious! Imagine introducing that as a classroom activity; not only do you have students laughing, but they're also practicing coordination and rhythm. Plus, who wouldn't want to impress their friends with their killer moves? "Hey, did you see Mr. U bust some moves? I think he needs to stick to the weight room."

Incorporating physical activity into education is a win-win situation. We're talking about better mental health, improved academic performance, and the development of lifelong habits. When students are sweating, laughing, and learning, we're creating an environment where they thrive. It's a beautiful thing to see! So, let's get those kids up, moving, and having a blast because trust me, nothing's more satisfying than watching them transform from sleepy marshmallows into energetic, glowing versions of themselves. And who knows? We might even sculpt the next great athlete-or at least someone who can win a Just Dance competition.

CREATING A FITNESS-FRIENDLY CLASSROOM

The elusive "fitness-friendly classroom." It's a space where the only weights students are lifting are their understanding of math, science, and English (well, that and maybe a few dozen pencils). As a retired cop now teaching special education, I recognized that not all students naturally adapt to a stagnant classroom environment where they're tethered to their desks like prisoners on a chain - minus the stripes, of course. After all, education doesn't need to resemble a solitary confinement experience; it should feel like an adventure! So how do we sprinkle in some physical activity without turning our classrooms into a chaotic gym foil of energy drinks and athletics shoes? Spoiler: it's all a matter of creativity!

First, let's start with the classroom layout. Think less of a traditional setup where rows of desks stare at the blackboard like you are in a Catholic School being taught by Sister Helen. Occasionally mix up the environment. Play with different set ups and see what works. Think about the physical activity and make a decision on what set up is best.

Now we know that this isn't something we would do every class every day. The importance of this section is to remind us that its ok to get kids up and moving. If your administration has a problem with this, then educate them on why you are doing it.

Next on the agenda for a fitness-friendly classroom: movement breaks. Let's face it; if one more student endures sitting for forty-five whole minutes while trying to comprehend the difference between "there," "their," and "they're," I might just need the handcuffs again to keep myself from losing control. Let's set an example and incorporate mini-movement sessions throughout the day! It could be a quick set of jumping jacks, a silly dance party, or even a brief "stand up if you can touch your toes" challenge. It'll break the monotony and make sure everyone is ready for the next wave of information. Bonus points if you make it competitive! I'm telling you, watching kids trying to out-squat each other is nothing short of comedy gold.

Now, let's chat about classroom resources. Instead of traditional textbooks, consider integrating activities like yoga or even meditation. My students may groan – at first, we all know teens can be drama queens - but what they'll discover in time is that a little mindful movement can actually aid focus. Picture a group of students trying out some quirky yoga poses. Sure, someone will inevitably fall over, and take down their partner in the process, but laughter will have them bouncing back up. Trust me; a giggle-filled classroom is marked by camaraderie - a breed of relationships that bodes well for community growth!

Let's not overlook the power of group work, either! Team projects are not just for academics; they can also be physical. Whether it's building a model or creating a presentation, include components that require the group to get up and move. Need to find data from different areas of the classroom? Send small teams on a "field trip" to scour the room. They'll love the excuse to stand up and move! Plus, you get extra stylish 'movin' and groovin' content in your classroom! A win-win!

Need proof? Do a demonstration or a fun exercise that reinforces the lesson at hand. Nothing builds teamwork better than trying to complete fun hurdles while discussing the scientific method! Your students will remember how they fell over trying to jump a "lava pit"-and will proudly recall the incident the next time they discuss cause and effect. If that's not an engaging lesson plan, I don't know what is!

Finally, above all, it's important to create an open dialogue about fitness and well-being. Engage students in discussions surrounding healthy habits and self-care. Remind them that mental and physical fitness go hand in hand, like peanut butter and jelly - or donuts and coffee! When they see you practicing what you preach - yes, even if it looks like an NFL player attempting ballet-they'll be inspired to embrace a fitness-friendly lifestyle.

With a few strategic efforts, we can morph the traditional classroom into a fitness-friendly haven. The goal is to create a space where movement is celebrated, laughter is bountiful, and the learning experience is energizing. So, let's get those students moving, sweating, and enjoying every moment of it; who knows? One day, they might just become the right fit for a future fitness revolution!

INCORPORATING MOVEMENT INTO LESSONS

As a former officer, I could tell you plenty of tales about chasing down suspects, but today we're focusing on something far more riveting: moving in class! As I often say to my students, "Sitting is for funerals and long waiting lines." This is not Aristotle's view on education-it's just a practical way to ensure our classrooms are lively, and our brains are buzzing instead of dozing off like a cat on a warm window ledge. The truth? Incorporating movement into lessons is an art form. It's like a dance routine, but instead of a spotlight and jazz hands, you get strokes of genius and a sprinkle of chaos.

Let's kick things off with something simple but effective: mind maps with a twist! Think of it as taking the concept of brainstorming to the next level. Gather your students around the board - so no one is just a passive observer - and get them physically involved in creating a mind map about a topic. Have them wander around, adding sticky notes, doodling ideas, or - because we all need some movement - doing an interpretive dance about their thoughts! Sure, it may not look like the rehearsal for a Broadway show, but watching Trevor flail his arms while shouting "Photosynthesis!" will be a sight to behold. Plus, it beats the deathly silence of kids staring blankly at their notes.

Let's strike a chord with math. Instead of solving problems seated at their desks (yawn), why not turn the classroom into a math relay race? Imagine this: scattering math problems around the room, and in teams, students must race to solve them. Not only do they get their heart rates up, but they also engage in some friendly competition. Because nothing pushes kids to success quite like the incentive of candy for the winning team! Trust me - it's the kind of math lesson that practically counts calories while counting beans. I co-taught a Algebra lesson with our Algebra teacher and it was our version of an escape room. Students were put into teams and had to solve problems throughout the room. The answers to each problem gave them a letter. Once all the letters were found, it gave them numbers to a combination lock box with candy. The kids loved this and the teamwork was incredible.

And let's transition to language arts! Students often struggle with writing, stuck in a headspace that feels as inspiring as a blank page. So why not do some "writing on the move"? Have them play word tag. One group goes to a designated area to grab a word or a phrase and returns to composition central, collaging sentences from their loot. If they're bolting around and their brains are firing on all cylinders, they'll leave classroom shyness behind. You know what they say: creativity flows when you're breaking a sweat! Or at least that's what I tell myself when I have the day's word scramble challenge looming.

Now, science class presents some fun opportunities as well.

When exploring concepts like gravity or motion, why teach it from the textbook when you can turn students into mini demonstrators? Grab some marbles, paper airplanes, or even water balloons because who doesn't love a little chaos in the name of learning? Let each team conduct an experiment, run it, and analyze its results. Combine it with motion to create an experience they'll not just remember but relish. Watching Ariana accidentally launch a water balloon into the principal's face while investigating projectile motion? That's going down in classroom lore, guaranteed!

History lessons can also embrace movement because let's be honest: nothing gets blood pumping like a historical reenactment. Who said you couldn't teach about the American Revolution while simultaneously turning the room into a battlefield? Students can choose roles, run from "British soldiers" (their friends, naturally, wearing red bandanas), and reenact memorable moments. Yes, it might look like a scene out of a badly staged historical play, but the nuance of feeling the heat of battle while recalling who threw the tea overboard? Irreplaceable!

Incorporating movement into lessons isn't just a quirky way to keep kids awake; it promotes engagement, camaraderie, and even a bit of joy in learning. With all the brain cells firing due to increased circulation, those "aha!" moments come easier. So tomorrow, when you see another student signed up for a nap in class, remember, unlocking creative movement might just turn those spaces into a vibrant circus of learning that even the toughest critic would rave about.

MEASURING SUCCESS: ASSESSING THE IMPACT OF FITNESS ON LEARNING

Measuring success - there's a phrase that can make teachers break into a cold sweat or bubble with excitement! In the world of education, measuring success typically involves spreadsheets, assessment tests, and possibly even a crystal ball for those predictive analytics. But in the pursuit of integrating fitness into our students' learning journey, assessing the impact of physical activity can be surprisingly fun. It's less about the numbers and more about the all-around joy and engagement in the classroom. So, let's grapple with this idea of measurement and the laughter that comes with it.

First let's face it, you can't measure the impact of fitness on learning with just one test on a Monday. If you've ever witnessed a teenage brain trying to wake up before noon, you'd understand! Instead, the measurement of success begins within the walls of engagement and enthusiasm. Take note of classroom participation. Are your students less inclined to zone out when you've incorporated movement into your lessons? Are they more likely to speak up and share ideas during a math sprint relay than during a two-hour lecture on the Pythagorean theorem? You bet! Observing that shift from "Who stole my pencil again?" utterance to "Wow, this is fun!" is success wrapped in a tortilla. As an example, let's tap into the idea of pre and post-activity reflections. When students participate in physical activity, have them jot down how they feel before and after. That's right! Keep those crayons and three-ring-binders close by because reflective journaling can become one of the simplest yet effective measurements of success. Did they feel more awake? Focused? Like they could launch themselves into space? The stories that emerge will likely be far more entertaining than mere results of a standardized test. Plus, you'll probably get a few giggles out of the doodles they draw to express their emotions.

Next, consider the correlation between fitness initiatives and their effects on mental health and behavior. Imagine framework where we look at the levels of stress, anxiety, and even social interactions of our students before they undergo fitness training versus after. You know, the ol' "this is not the best day" vs. "look at me, I've discovered endorphins!" Creating a pre and post-test situation with self-assessment tools can paint a picture of how movements affect emotional well-being. Students might say they feel more capable of dealing with stress or encountering social dilemmas differently. The before-and-after transformation from a grumpy teenager into a more relaxed, open-minded "social octopus" can dramatically illustrate the unique impacts of getting those hip flexors warmed up.

Let's not overlook academic performance; though, I can already hear the groans. Sure, standardized testing is widely disappointing and brain-mushing but comparing academic performance over time - and factoring in physical activity levels -

can provide valuable insight. It's like finding where your socks disappear in the dryer - a mystery that needs solving! Track changes from the beginning to the end of the semester to see if there's a noticeable uptick in grades or comprehension. When you see students improving because of their involvement with fitness, it's groundbreaking.

At the end of the day, remembering to assess various metrics to measure success in a fitness-friendly learning environment is paramount. It's less about the rigid data and more about the burst of positivity, enthusiasm, and creativity that comes from movement-infused classes. As educators, we want to make sure we're skipping along the path of success, not endlessly racing to the finish line. So, whether it's engaging personal reflections, noticeable changes in behavior, or perhaps an art showcase of the best doodles about feelings after exercising, embrace the wild ride of laughter that comes with measuring the delightful impact of fitness on learning.

PART TWELVE
EMBRACING DIVERSITY IN SCHOOLS

THE IMPORTANCE OF CULTURAL AWARENESS

Cultural awareness, my friends, is The name of the game! If you've ever walked into a high school and felt like you've just entered a United Nations meeting without a translator, then you can appreciate the importance of being culturally aware. Understanding the diverse backgrounds of our students isn't just about being politically correct; it's about being able to dodge those tricky cultural landmines that could turn a normal school day into an episode of Survivor: Classroom Edition. Forget about navigating the complexities of lesson plans - first, we need to acknowledge the cast of characters we're working with, and trust me, they come with their unique plot twists.

Imagine this: You're trying to teach a physics lesson on gravity, and you go into a detailed explanation about how every action has an equal and opposite reaction-A wonderfully articulate way to explain why Jimmy should rethink jumping off the school roof with a makeshift parachute. But before you even get to the part where he ends up declaring himself "King of Physics," little did you know that one of your students, Juan, is not simply pondering the laws of gravity but is nervously wondering if discussing his family's culture-a melting pot of traditions-will end with him becoming a human science experiment. Suddenly, the lesson plan becomes less about Newton and more about the dozens of ways we fail to appreciate one another's realities.

Cultural awareness is about recognizing these nuances in our classrooms. It's understanding that each student's story shapes how they learn, interact, and respond to authority figures like yours truly. Believe me; even the term "authority figure" sends shivers down the spine of some teenagers when it comes from an ex-cop like me. We ought to remember that some students may come from backgrounds that view law enforcement with skepticism, while others may idolize them based on their community experiences. The last thing I want is for them to think of me as the enemy while attempting to figure out if multiplication is still the same regardless of where you come from.

If you thought teaching was solely about shoving ideas down students' throats like I'm feeding them vegetables at lunch time, think again! Every day in the classroom is a teeter-totter of culture and communication. Without that critical element, we become like a high school band where everyone plays a different tune, and you can bet it ends with someone crying into their lunch tray. As educators, we must listen and allow cultural backgrounds to enrich classroom discussions rather than stifle them with a "one-size-fits-all" approach.

Picture yourself in a classroom, trying to bring unity to your diverse ensemble. You call for silence with the same vigor as a traffic cop during rush hour, and what do you get? A chorus of "But Mr. U, I can't help it if my family celebrates a different holiday every week!" Well, isn't that the truth! It's all about embracing these differences. Instead of shutting down conversations about varied festivities, let's use them as teaching moments. You can teach math through cookie decorating while celebrating Diwali or explore science through the physics of fireworks during the Lunar New Year. Because who doesn't love math and explosions, right?

Every day is an opportunity to model cultural appreciation. Students need to see that their backgrounds matter. They need to know that their stories heighten their worth and could be the perfect catalyst to help others learn and grow. And you better bet I remind them that if you're not part of the solution by bringing your culture into the conversation, you're as useful as a screen door on a submarine!

Never underestimate the power of cultural awareness. It's not as simple as giving students a bland, tasteless noodle dish called "multiculturalism." Instead, make it a delicious feast where everyone brings a dish to the table! The more we engage with our students, the more we understand that this potluck of perspectives will not only keep our classrooms vibrant but may even earn us a few unexpected "thanks" from students. In the end, cultural awareness is about elevating students and providing them with a platform to share their unique experiences. Let's get our classrooms bubbling with excitement and knowledge by navigating those differences with a sense of humor. After all, learning should always leave you feeling a little lighter, like a snack after leg day at the weight room.

STRATEGIES FOR INCLUSIVE CLASSROOMS

When it comes to creating inclusive classrooms, I gotta tell you, it feels a bit like trying to untangle a giant mass of Christmas lights just before the holiday season - entertainingly chaotic but potentially fraught with unexpected shocks! Still, I assure you that the effort is worth it. Don't let the extra wiring of backgrounds, experiences, and learning styles feel like a tangled mess; instead, let's treat it like an opportunity to dazzle our students with an educational light show that even the Grinch couldn't resist.

The first strategy in my tool kit is differentiation. Differentiation is not just a fancy educational jargon that I throw around like I'm in a TEDx Talk; it's the art of tailoring instruction to meet our students' varied needs. Consider this: some students may learn best by hearing you drone on (my voice has been professionally tuned for such occasions), while others may require visual aids to keep their attention longer than the duration of a sneeze. If you can incorporate multimedia presentations, hands-on activities, and group discussions all while dodging single, flying paper airplanes, you're doing something right! Remember, it's about being accommodating, not becoming a human pretzel while attempting to please everyone. Find what works for your students, and soon you'll be the circus master instead of the unsuspecting lion!

Next up is cultivating a classroom environment where every voice matters. I mean, who wouldn't want to hear Kevin's fantastic ideas about why we should outlaw high school cafeteria food? The easiest way to make every student feel valued is to foster an atmosphere of respect and encourage participation. Even the shyest flower in the garden will bloom if given a little sunlight, or in our case, opportunities to shine. Implementing structured discussions or small group collaborations can turn the most reluctant students into the leading voices of classroom democracy. Have students share their thoughts and feedback. By promoting inclusive participation, you help students feel like they're part of the tapestry instead of a misplaced thread on the floor.

One of my personal favorites is employing cooperative learning strategies. Think of this as putting your students in a group workout session - everyone sweats, everyone struggles, and nothing strengthens friendships faster than surviving a shared "Death by Math" workout. You're not just enforcing collaboration to create group projects where one person does all the work while the rest binge-watch TikTok. Instead, you're creating an environment where they can all contribute their skills toward a shared goal. Pairing students with different strengths and weaknesses fosters connections and cultivates a culture of empathy and understanding. Plus, who wouldn't want to high-five their buddy after finishing a project when the world has been plagued with enough negativity?

Don't forget about adapting your materials and resources! Imagine walking into the classroom and witnessing a beautifully organized library that rivals that of a cozy bookstore. In that lovely literary haven, students can choose books in various formats that cater to their learning preferences. Why limit options when you can have audiobooks, graphic novels, and good ol' printed wonders all on the same shelf? Providing diverse materials not only supports different learning styles but also exposes students to multiple cultural perspectives. An inclusive library where they can grab a book on the adventures of a young girl in Somalia and then switch over to a tale of struggling through high school in the U.S. expands their world while sparking discussions that can blow even the stuffiest classrooms wide open.

Lastly, let's always return to the power of building relationships. Notice those "sensitive" students who might be lurking in the back with the freshest pair of sneakers? They might not give you eye contact, but that doesn't mean they aren't absorbing the environment. A foundational piece of inclusion is building trust and rapport. Check in with your students daily, know their hobbies, and pay attention to their lives outside the four walls of academic madness. There's a difference between an educator and a mere knowledge dispenser, and those who can connect personally with students will likely work harder because they don't want to disappoint that teacher.

When you put these strategies into practice, you'll be well on your way to creating a vibrant and inclusive classroom where all students feel respected, heard, and supported. Just like in weightlifting, where you start light and gradually add more weight, approach inclusivity methodically. With patience, effort, and a sense of humor, you'll empower your students to flex their own strengths, turning your classroom into a place where everyone can grow like weeds - beautiful, colorful weeds. So, get ready to untangle those classroom lights and shine bright like a freshly polished trophy!

CREATING CULTURALLY RELEVANT CURRICULUM

The culturally relevant curriculum: the elusive jackalope of education that makes every educator feel like they're trying to catch a rainbow with a butterfly net. But hang onto your hats, because crafting a curriculum that resonates with students from diverse backgrounds isn't just a lofty ideal-it's the secret recipe for unlocking engagement, creativity, and a little street credit among those snickering in the back row. Creating this curriculum is akin to whipping up the perfect blend of spices for chili; you need just the right ingredients to make it hot enough to sizzle while keeping everyone comfortably satisfied at the same time.

Let's start off with quite possibly the most absurd revelation: KNOW YOUR STUDENTS! I know, I know - this is groundbreaking stuff! You won't win any innovative teaching awards for just telling yourself that, but understanding your students' backgrounds, interests, cultures, and experiences lays the essential foundation for a curriculum that truly connects. Think of it like a friendly neighborhood party - nobody wants to show up to a barbecue where there's nothing but lettuce and water. What if we found out that Kim's family celebrates Kwanzaa and Sarah's parents are into elaborate Lunar New Year festivities? Well incorporate that knowledge into your lessons! A social studies unit on cultural celebrations could turn into a lively exploration of family traditions and spiritual significance - complete with pineapple fried rice for lunch.

Another critical recipe for a culturally relevant curriculum is representation. So, if you're still teaching the same tired, age-old literature lists from your high school days, it's time for some serious updates! A rich curriculum is one that includes voices and perspectives that reflect the diversity of the student body. Imagine the joy of your students when they encounter authors from a variety of cultures, backgrounds, and identities! I'm talking about shaking it up and reading works by those inspired by their own experiences. Not only does this validate students' identities, but it also helps them understand the broader world.

Let's also throw in real world connections! I've seen it too many times: a teacher stands at the front, passionately lecturing about topics that feel utterly disconnected from students' lives. Because let's be honest, high school life can be as perplexing and complicated as trying to solve a Rubik's cube while blind-folded. To bridge that gap, create lessons that incorporate local events, historical context, and contemporary issues. For example, while discussing environmental science, encourage students to explore local impacts on their community. When students recognize the relevance of what they are learning, they'll engage more deeply.

Let's talk about flexibility! In education, flexibility is key. A culturally relevant curriculum requires us to adapt our material and teaching strategies according to students' comfort levels and needs. If a student shares a unique experience or perspective, seize that moment, and adjust your lesson to allow deeper conversation. This not only cultivates a sense of community, but also empowers students to recognize their own capabilities as contributing members of the learning environment.

Now, here's the kicker: adding creativity and fun into the mix! Engage your students with hands-on projects, technology, and artistic exploration. Instead of rote memorization, encourage creativity through art, drama, or digital storytelling. A geography lesson about unique landscape features can easily transform into a project where students create 3D models of their favorite world landmarks.

Lastly, let's remember the power of reflection. Catching the Little League spirit, let's reminisce about how each lesson went and encourage student feedback on the curriculum itself. After all, if students feel like they have ownership in the learning process, they are more likely to contribute actively to class discussions. So, don't be afraid to ask them what they think! It's not just some promotional contest, it's about creating a dynamic and responsive classroom environment.

So here we are, at the vibrant finish line of cultural relevance in curriculum design! When you create a culturally relevant curriculum, you're igniting sparks of enthusiasm, encouraging empathy, and preparing students for the global world beyond your classroom. As we embrace these challenges head-on, let's keep the fact that laughter-and perhaps a little confusion-might ensue. But that's perfectly okay! After all, education should be as fulfilling as a well-balanced meal. Let's get to building that perfect blend of flavors, relationships, and, yes, even a dash of delicious chaos!

PART THIRTEEN
PARENTAL INVOLVEMENT: A TEAM EFFORT

THE IMPORTANCE OF COMMUNICATION WITH PARENTS

When it comes to the educational landscape, communication with parents is akin to having a secret weapon in your back pocket, like a retired cop hiding an unmarked donut. It's not just nice-to-have; it's essential. If you think about it, every teacher can pretty much agree on one thing: parents are like those plot twists you never saw coming in a movie. Parents can be often shocking, frequently entertaining, and sometimes downright unbelievable. Communication plays a pivotal role, smooths out rough patches, and turns "helicopter parenting" into a well-coordinated drone strike where everyone lands safely.

First off, there's two types of parents. We have parents who are genuinely interested in their kid's school experience, and they have their own special radar to sniff out everything from a runny nose to a classroom scuffle. Honestly, sometimes they have more intel than I did as a cop! If there's something fishy going down in the school, you can bet that parents will hear about it faster than you can say "School lunch meat loaf, I want it now"!! By establishing a reliable line of communication, we can stay ahead of any rumors, provide context, and keep the channels open for discussion.

The other type of parent is the parent who does not want to be a part of their child's education. These types of parents are the most difficult. They typically don't return emails or phone calls. They set-up meetings and don't show. This is especially frustrating in the special education role because there are a lot of things we need consent for. If we don't hear back from a parent to hold a meeting, just give them a phone call stating that their child is not going to graduate. Watch these parents crawl out of the woodwork. In our digital age, we have various tools at our disposal for communication. Emails, texts, the occasional smoke signal; you name it, parents are using it! Digital platforms have the potential to be both a blessing and a curse. Sure, it's great that I can update parents when their child has achieved something remarkable, like pulling off that astonishing feat of getting through a week without losing a single homework assignment. But if you think I'm only going to use it for good news, think again! I wield that power like a former cop who just discovered donuts - it can go in either direction at the speed of light!

What hits the spot even more is personalized communication. Asking a parent about their kid's latest obsession be it TikTok dances or whatever's trending in gaming- helps promote rapport. They might not want to hear about quadratic equations, but they'll gladly listen to you discussing their little one's newfound obsession with slime. A tip from a retiree: when you relate to parents about their children's interests, it builds trust and opens up channels of communication. It's like saying, "Hey, I might have an arrest record, but I also have excellent taste in things that bubble." You've got to show that you're not just here for the test scores, but for the holistic development of their child.

But communication isn't just a one-way street; it's more like navigating a car chase! It requires weaving in and out of traffic, anticipating roadblocks, and dodging the occasional stray dog, especially with parents involved. Getting feedback from parents is incredibly valuable. It directly bears on the success of a student. When parents feel involved, they are more likely to share concerns and insights that might help us as educators ensure that each child has their best foot forward. They observe things we may not see in the classroom - like what happens when their teenager returns home and transforms into a couch potato scrolling endlessly through social media.

Fun fact: many of my most memorable lessons in communication have come from parents giving me a heads-up about their child's behavior that even the best disguises couldn't hide!

Ultimately, the takeaway is simple: open, honest, and humorous communication with parents fosters strong partnerships that enhance student success. It creates goodwill and breaks down barriers, mirroring how trust is built in law enforcement but with fewer donuts on the table. So, let's keep those lines of communication wide open! Just like in the force, working hand in hand with families will always lead us to brighter days and better outcomes for our students.

CREATING A WELCOMING ENVIRONMENT FOR FAMILIES

Creating a welcoming environment for families in schools is one of those honorable missions that bring to mind everything from hosting a family barbecue to soothing a parent who just found out their child is missed 23 assignments in English. As someone who transitioned from the world of policing to teaching, I've seen the kind of havoc that confusion and tension can wreak in a community. Think of schools as classrooms but with more awkward moments and a lot more hormones. When families feel welcome, they are more inclined to participate in classroom activities and contribute to a positive atmosphere.

Let's talk about that front office. You know, the first-place parents see when they enter the school. It's like tourists walking into the Grand Canyon. If we want parents to feel welcomed, we need to transform that space from a sterile, uninviting room resembling a police interrogation chamber into a vibrant, friendly place. Imagine smiling and decorations that would make even Hallmark proud. Colorful pictures and posters, maybe even a wall of student artwork - you get the idea. It's the little touches that make entering the school feel like a hug instead of a checkpoint!

Next, let's consider the language we use when communicating with families. If I have learned anything from my career in law enforcement, it is that technical jargon often confuses people faster than trying to explain quantum physics while handcuffed in a car's backseat. Just as police reports should be devoid of unnecessary lingo, communication with families should be straightforward, and friendly. We should aim for clarity and warmth, so they feel comfortable reaching out for help or with questions. If we want parents to engage, let's ditch the educational jargon that makes them feel like they stepped into a foreign language class!

Another vital aspect is accessibility. We need to accommodate a variety of needs, especially when it comes to different languages spoken at home. Schools should offer translation services and, if possible, bilingual staff. It's heartbreaking to think of a family feeling unwelcome because they have to decipher an English-only newsletter. Treat it like a police intervention where everyone deserves to be heard, understood, and welcomed, no matter the language barrier! Conversations should be relaxed, inviting, and devoid of off-putting over-analysis; you know, the awkward kind that makes you doubt your abilities.

The physical environment speaks volumes too. A welcoming school can be as vibrant and lively as a community potluck, and I'm not just saying that because I'm hungry. Comfortable seating areas, vibrant colors, and even snacks can make a world of difference. Honestly, who wouldn't want to walk into a school lobby that smells like freshly baked cookies? Nothing says "welcome" like a pleasantly suspicious aroma wafting through the air, right? Kids and parents alike will be scampering towards that place like excited velociraptors!

We should also consider family events as opportunities to connect. Parents shouldn't feel like they're walking into a high-stakes negotiation. Family nights, BBQs, or even game nights in the gym can foster a relaxed atmosphere. Imagine everything I mentioned coming together to create an event where everyone feels included, from those parents who glow with pride, to those who may not know what a "halftime show" is. Slip in the joyous encounters of strong community engagement, and you're bound to inspire a family allegiance that looks a little less like a pact with a mafia boss and more like a potluck reunion.

Lastly, never underestimate the power of good old-fashioned humor. Just as I've learned during my time in the police force, laughter can diffuse tensions faster than you can say "bad donut." A light-hearted joke or a playful banter goes a long way in creating warmth between families and educators. Sure, it might get a few eye rolls, but who doesn't love a fun conversation.

In summary, creating a welcoming environment for families isn't rocket science; it's about genuine effort. With a friendly office atmosphere, approachable language, accessibility, enticing physical spaces, engaging events, and a touch of humor, we can build bonds with families that lead to supportive partnerships. Trust me, as a retired cop who's now a special education teacher, I know that feeling of trust and security can calm even the toughest group of parents in a matter of minutes. Let's turn those hesitant visitors into enthusiastic participants, one warm interaction at a time!

STRATEGIES FOR EFFECTIVE PARENT-TEACHER CONFERENCES

Parent-teacher conferences: the annual ritual where teachers put on their best brave faces and parents practice their various "concerned" looks. This is the one time each year where we all gather together in what sometimes resembles an awkward dance party - minus the partying and all the awkwardness. As a retired police officer who now roams the hallowed halls of academia as a special education teacher, I have maneuvered through the wild world of parent-teacher conferences enough times to tell you that there's an art to making these interactions productive, engaging, and almost enjoyable. Let's dive into some strategies that make it less of an interrogation and more like a casual chat over coffee.

First and foremost, preparation is key. Think of it like getting ready for an undercover operation; you wouldn't want to stroll into a drug house looking like you've just woken up from a nap. Parents want to know that you've done your homework. Begin by gathering and organizing relevant materials and data on each student - test scores, participation records, and any insights into their classroom experiences. Having a few "highlight reels." Snippets about their child can go a long way in breaking the ice and steering the conversation in a positive direction. Prepare to share anecdotes, progress markers, and, of course, little quirks that make each kid delightfully unique! Whether it's that amazing art project they did or their newfound passion for mathematics. Let the parents know that their kid also does good things in class.

Next, setting the mood can make a world of difference. Picture this: a dimly lit conference room with mood lighting, a scent reminiscent of vanilla candles filling the air, and soft jazz playing in the background. Okay, reality check; that might not be feasible, but we can definitely add warmth to the environment in other ways. Get creative! Use student artwork as decorations or provide a comfy seating arrangement. Having water bottles or snacks available can ease the nerves and act as a pleasant distraction as parents wait. When they come into a welcoming atmosphere, parents tend to relax, and that comfort will ultimately lead to a smoother.

Communicating with parents should feel like a partnership, not an inquisition. Start the conference by reinforcing your genuine interest in their child's well-being and development. A friendly approach helps set the tone and reassures parents that you're on their side. Our goal should be to invite parents into the dialogue rather than back them into a corner like startled criminals. Ask open-ended questions like, "What are your thoughts on how things are going at home?" or "How does your child feel about school?" This empowers parents to share their insights. Think of it like conducting an investigation - not the police kind, but rather where you're uncovering treasures of information that could help better understand the student's environment.

While discussing any areas for improvement, lead with constructive feedback rather than criticism. Lay the foundation by emphasizing the positives first, like the impressive way Johnny leads the classroom's gym exercises or how Sarah's contributions to class discussions are nothing short of stellar. Then gently pivot to the areas that need work, framing them as opportunities for growth. Empathy goes a long way here, allowing parents to feel less defensive and be more receptive.

Another effective strategy is followed through just as a good cop doesn't leave a case unsolved, we don't want our conferences to be one sided. Make sure to establish a clear plan for follow steps after the meeting is over.

Will you share resources or tools they can use at home? Will you check in with the student to help address any specific concerns? Keep the dialogue going with parents, assuring them that you'll continue to monitor their child's progress. Believe me: establishing an ongoing communication channel will turn parents into collaborative partners in the best way possible.

In summary, effective parent-teacher conferences don't have to feel like a high-stakes interrogation. By preparing thoughtfully, setting a welcoming mood, communicating, emphasizing strengths, and ensuring follow through, we can create an environment that fosters connection, understanding, and collaboration. It's essential that we recognize the power of building strong relationships with families. After all, we're ll on this wild ride together - teachers, parents, and children alike - and ultimately, it's about creating a supportive ecosystem for our students to flourish. And let's be real: a little extra happy energy never hurt anyone. So, let's spice up those conferences and make them something to remember!

PART FOURTEEN
HANDLING DISCIPLINE WITH CARE

UNDERSTANDING THE PURPOSE OF DISCIPLINE

Discipline! That magical word chat sends shivers down the spines of students and brings delight to some teachers who secretly revel in their authoritative roles. Discipline in schools serves a vital purpose, yet it is often misunderstood. As a retired cop who has transitioned into the teaching world, I've come to realize discipline isn't just about constantly waving the proverbial "handcuffs" in the air. It's a symphony of structure and freedom, expectations and expressions, and sometimes, it's akin to flashing a red piece of cloth in front of a bull's face.

So, first things first: what is the purpose of discipline? When we hear the word, many envision detention halls filled with kids who somehow thought that a jaunty jump off the cafeteria tables was a great idea. But discipline is actually rooted in the desire to foster a productive environment where students can learn, grow, and potentially, just potentially, make fewer questionable decisions. It helps set the boundaries that guide behavior and provides a framework for acceptable conduct. Think of it as the GPS for young minds navigating the chaotic route through high school. If you stray too far off course, your metaphorical car might find itself in a ditch, covered in soda cans and axe body spray.

Moreover, discipline is not merely about punishment; it's about accountability. Sure, kids will misbehave and while the natural inclination might be to slap the nearest detention slip onto their foreheads, the goal should instead be to teach them a sense of responsibility. I mean, can anybody plan to get through life without understanding the consequences? We aren't prepping them for a career of 'professional procrastinators', are we? Discipline guides students in making choices, often referencing the classic "think before you act" mantra. Let's face it, if you can dodge responsibility in high school, just imagine the super-human ways kids will find to avoid adulthood.

Also, here's a revelation: discipline can actually help form relationships between students and teachers. In my years as a special education teacher, I've seen how setting parameters fosters mutual respect. I have a student who dumps all of his "stuff" in my office. By stuff I mean a backpack, gym bag, two pairs of shoes, his lunch box, a bag of snacks, and a skateboard – which is still in my office. He obviously doesn't want to carry all that crap around with him, so as much as I get tired of seeing it, I let him use my office. Students want to know you care, but they also need to comprehend that there are limits to acceptable behavior. Think of it as establishing a perimeter around a prized vegetable garden - you want those tomatoes to flourish without being trampled by rambunctious deer. When students understand that our disciplinary actions stem from a place of caring rather than hatred for their "stuff", they respond positively. Suddenly, we're not just background figures in their lives; we're authority figures who genuinely impact their growth.

Of course, if we want students to respect the rules, those rules need to be fair. Yes, fair! It's a lofty concept that often grazes the heads of rulers like a flat-footed gymnast missing her vault. Discipline isn't about a one-size-fits-all approach. Every child is unique, and their context must be considered. Why did Timmy throw his shoe in class? Perhaps he was simply trying to express his creativity - or trying to distract from the fact that he forgot to do his homework. Understanding behavior allows us to vary our responses instead of turning every minor infraction into an episode where Timmy ends up in academic solitary confinement.

Restorative practices also play a vital role in understanding the purpose of discipline. Rather than reducing students merely to their misdeeds, this approach encourages us to explore the root cause of their actions. Did Angela chew gum in class because she's secretly auditioning to be the next big YouTube star with a bubble-blowing competition? Did Pedro act out because he didn't comprehend a lesson and was too embarrassed to ask for help? Addressing behaviors holistically reminds us that we're not just dealing with little miscreants; we're educators helping young people evolve into responsible citizens and optimistic adults.

When we truly understand the purpose of discipline, it transforms from a burden into a tool: a way to build a thriving classroom culture. Healthy discipline encourages reflection, guides choices, and, ideally, doesn't involve ice packs or the school nurse too frequently. As both a former lawman and current educator, my journey through the hallways has led me to discover that a disciplined but caring environment isn't simply a method of getting students to comply; it's about helping them flourish, one lesson - and one cell phone at a time.

FAIR AND CONSISTENT CONSEQUENCES

The age-old quest for fairness! It's the holy grail of teaching, and when it comes to consequences in the classroom, it's practically the Excalibur we all yearn to wield. In a world where your students may believe they're auditioning for "Survivor: High School Edition," nothing brings more chaos than inconsistent consequences. When you have new administration who comes in and on his agenda in enforcing policies, then admin needs to include the staff. It's not a matter of an email. There needs to be an in-person staff meeting. Unfortunately, most new admins want the control and have an "it's my show" attitude. Zero tolerance works in some scenarios, but when you are talking about students with IEPs or 504 plans, it's no longer a black and white policy. There is always a gray area. Hint Hint: special ed kids have this thing called an IEP (Individualized Education Plan). Within that IEP there's this thing called a "behavior intervention plan (BIP)." Hate to break it to all you new administrators. Before you start suspending a special education kid you better open that IEP and look for a BIP. You fail to do this, and you will have a Due Process meeting on your hands faster than you can say "vape pen!"

Back to consistency: Think about it, if David gets a slap on the wrist for using a slingshot to launch spitballs, but Zak ends up facing a trial by fire for doodling in his notebook, you've opened a Pandora's box of mistrust and anarchy. I mean, how can we expect our young scholars to adhere to the rules when the rulebook appears to change based on which teacher had their coffee spilled that morning? Now if a student doesn't have a behavior intervention plan, then consistency is key. It may require a little research into the IEP, but it will save you a world of headache.

So, what does it mean to have fair and consistent consequences? First off, it implies that we're not playing favorites like a high school prom king or queen. Seriously, who wants to be that teacher whom students regard with the same disdain they have for a broken pencil sharpener? When students know they can expect a certain level of response no matter who is in charge, it creates a sense of stability. I like to envision my classroom as a place everyone is treated to the same recipe for success, whether it's a triple-shot mocha or a simple cup o' joe. Consistent consequences mean students feel they are more likely to receive a straight-up answer rather than a cryptic riddle that resembles something out of a Shakespearean play - a swirling mystery that leaves them baffled as to why they ended up in detention when all they did was laugh a little too hard at a bad dad joke. However, consistent consequences don't mean we've got to toss an iron fist at every tiny infraction. Just like I can't throw the book at a kid for forgetting to turn in their paper, we need to take context into account. A freshman dressing up for spirit day and sporting bright yellow shoelaces while doing a jig in the cafeteria should not automatically face the guillotine, but instead politely asked him to save the performance for the school talent show. Recognizing the nuances of each situation ensures no one becomes a victim of an ill-timed 'overreaction' - think of it as teaching them not just about rules, but emotional intelligence.

Let's not forget the beauty of transparency. When consequences are as transparent as a pair of awkwardly oversized glasses, students are more likely to respect and understand them. Kids will push boundaries-it's practically in their DNA. They might roll their eyes at the rules you articulate, but when those rules are clear and the consequences are visible, it sets the stage for something remarkable: a united classroom community! This means getting those dear students involved in discussions on rules and consequences, so we're not reverting to ancient punishment methods. We want to avoid situations where they figure, "Hey, if Mr. U doesn't mind dodging my spitball shot, surely, he means I can fire a few more!"

Moreover, consistency sets the foundation for teaching accountability. When consequences are uniformly applied, students start realizing that their actions have weight.

In my travels through the myriad minefields called high schools, I've learned that maintaining fairness and consistency in consequences is like running a great relay race: you pass the baton of guidance and its now in the student's hands. Fairness makes for a safe environment where students can thrive - free of the confusion of erratic consequences that can feel more arbitrary than deciding what toppings belong on pizza.

So, as you embrace the whimsical chaos of the classroom, remember that the true strength of teaching lies not just in handing out consequences like candy on Halloween. Instead, it's ·about establishing a structure that supports creativity, responsibility, and - who'd have thought it? - a smidge of common sense. Consistent consequences are crucial in farming a thriving learning landscape-one where students flourish rather than flounder, and we get to navigate this wild ride with a hearty laugh and maybe even some sweet dance moves along the way.

THE ROLE OF COMMUNICATION IN DISCIPLINE

Communication-the often-underappreciated magic wand we as educators have at our disposal! It's the essential ingredient in the recipe for effective discipline, yet somehow, it often gets overshadowed by the grand spectacle of flashy classroom management tactics and the occasional desperate appeal to the "please don't make me resort to sending you to the principal" card. I spent years enforcing the law and trust me, communication was key in getting people to understand that no, they can't park in the no-parking zone "just for a second." The same principle applies in the classroom. Without it, we're just a bunch of well-meaning teachers waving our arms like the directors of a disastrous school play - who can't remember their lines and don't actually know what the production is about anyway.

So why exactly is ·communication critical in discipline? For starters, it's the bridge that connects educators to students. Without that bridge, we risk leaving students stranded on an island of confusion, wondering whether they should fear the wrath of the classroom or embrace it like it's an eagerly anticipated game of dodgeball. When our students misbehave - or, let's just say, "explore their improvisational skills in unexpected ways"-the communication that follows is crucial to clarify expectations and consequences. We need to discuss what exactly went wrong and why the noble act of launching a paper airplane during a lecture may need to be dialed down from an "exhilarating science project" to "you did not make a great decision."

Moreover, if we want our students to respect disciplinary actions, they must first understand the reasoning behind them. This doesn't mean delivering a monologue worthy of an Oscar for every tiny infraction, though I often get the theatrical urge when explaining why it's frowned upon to call the new substitute teacher by his facial hair, "mustache." It means framing our dialogues in ways that leverage their youthful instincts. Engaging students in a manner that feels relatable-using analogies or memes they might chuckle at - can illuminate the connection between their actions and the consequences. Wouldn't you agree? Imagine explaining the blinking red devil face on the principal's office door is like a warning signal that they should consider their choices before acting on that impulse.

Now, let's address the infamous "tone." Yes, I said it - the five-letter word that can make or break a conversation. Your tone can convey whether you're serious or just trying to channel your inner stand-up comedian. Picture this: you're explaining to a student why they can't wear a Hawaiian lei to class as though it's an essential fashion accessory, and you have to ensure your tone resonates with authority and understanding rather than descending into the chaos of half-hearted humor. Using a blend of empathy and firmness.

Let's not forget the role of active listening in communication. Now, I know what you're thinking: "Josh, we're navigating the jungle of teenage minds - how can we actively listen to individuals who often speak in a dialect of emojis?" A valid observation! But here's the kicker: making an effort to genuinely listen to a student can yield huge dividends. If Melissa insists on explaining that they did throw a paper airplane because the "physics of flight is relevant to our learning," then take that opportunity to delve deeper into their reasoning. This gives them the chance to voice themselves while allowing you to gently steer the conversation back to the lesson at hand. Suddenly, you're revealing the exciting world of physics while establishing a line of communication that fosters trust rather than distrust.

EVALUATING DISCIPLINE POLICIES AND THEIR IMPACT

Evaluating discipline policies! It's like getting your teeth checked at the dentist: necessary, but you never look forward to it. Most folks would rather binge-watch reruns of a two-hour lecture about paint drying than dive into the complexities of discipline policies in schools. However, if we want to foster an environment where students feel safe, respected, and capable of learning - while avoiding surprise food lights reminiscent of a food-related reality show-we absolutely must assess how our discipline practices are functioning (or not).

When it comes to evaluating discipline policies, we need to ask ourselves the essential questions: Are these policies really being enforced as intended? Do they promote fairness, growth, and accountability, or do they serve as a lovely paperweight on some dusty shelf in the teacher's lounge? An effective evaluation process should include gathering data on the number and types of disciplinary actions taken. If you find your records looking more chaotic, it may be time to pivot your approach. We want data that shines brightly, reflecting the reality of the students' experiences, rather than a nebulous fog of vague infractions that leave us wondering who's getting punished for what.

It's essential to not only look at the discipline data but also at the impact those policies have on students' overall behavior and engagement. Has there been an increase in student suspensions? Are attendance rates plummeting faster than a group of students running from a surprise pop quiz? If disciplinary actions are resulting in increased disengagement from the educational process, we might have some adjustments to make. An observed rise in disciplinary cases, particularly among specific demographic groups, can also hint at underlying issues that need our attention.

We need to analyze whether our policies are inadvertently harming students instead helps students see that you genuinely care while still demanding respect for classroom norms. Law enforcement has what's called the use of force continuum. Police use this when it comes to dealing with the general public. While some departments are moving away from this strategy, it can still serves as a use of force guide for the officers who still believe in it. Even though it is a step ladder to using force, there is nothing that says you have to follow the steps in order. For example, the bottom of the ladder is officer presence. This is showing up on scene and looking the part. Do you look like a formidable presence, or do you look like you couldn't fight your way out of a wet paper bag? Now if the suspect pulls a knife, you don't have to go through all the other steps before drawing your gun. The golden rule is to always stay one up on the suspect. In teaching, we don't have this guide because we don't carry pepper spray, a taser, a baton, or a gun. Our only weapons we have in the classroom are teacher presence and communication.

Let me explain, by presence I mean looking professional and acting like you are in charge even if you have no clue what you're doing. Stand with confidence and take a deep breath. It's your class not theirs. By communication I mean de-escalation or verbal judo. Your tone during these two techniques will make or break you. You cannot resort to a hidden taser that's in our desk or a chancla in the closet. I have been through a dozen trainings on use of force and if teachers are not comfortable using verbal judo or de-escalation techniques, then they better find another means to calm a situation that could erupt any minute. Bottom line is that if you can communicate to your students, you will sweat confidence, and the classroom will be yours.

Guiding them toward better behavior. When evaluating policies, we also ought to consider staff and student voices. As some administrators forget, this isn't merely a dictatorship of the adults! Engaging students and staff in the evaluation process can yield unexpected insights. Students can provide valuable information on how they view discipline and its effectiveness. Staff needs to have input because they are the ones in the trenches! They know what works and what doesn't. They know their students better than the administration. If you exclude the staff, your perfect discipline policies are gonna be flushed down the toilet. During the staff and student evaluation of the policies, allow them to have input on if they feel that the consequences fit the crime?

That feedback helps validate their experiences and demonstrates that their voices matter - something often lost when administrators rule with an iron stapler. Gather their opinions on how they perceive the fairness and effectiveness of discipline measures; you'd be surprised what a little feedback from old and young minds can reveal about your classroom culture.

Equally important is to provide educators with training and resources to understand and apply these policies effectively. I can't tell you how many times I've seen teachers get tangled in the complexities of implementing discipline without adequate support. By providing educators with professional development around discipline policies and positively reinforcing strategies, we enable them to implement discipline that's effective and constructive rather than punitive. You want them to feel like superheroes equipped with emotional intelligence rather than feeling helpless because they are confused on what to do.

Evaluation doesn't stop at data collection and feedback loops-it's a continuous cycle. The best part about assessing discipline policies is the opportunity for refinement. Think of this as your classroom's very own annual "tune-up." Regularly revisiting your policies allows you to respond to the evolving needs of your students and creates an adaptable framework for learning. Whether it's clarifying a vague rule that students seem to interpret differently depending on whether it's Monday or Friday or reimagining your approach based on trends. Effectiveness will improve with consistent evaluation. As we refine and update our practices, we create a living discipline system rather than a museum exhibit behind glass.

Lastly, let's not forget the fundamental truth that the impact of discipline policies ultimately reflects in a school's culture. Are students thriving and engaged, or do they seem like family dogs on the brink of being sent to the dog park for a "mental health escape"? The vibe of a school is infectious. Educators, staff, and administrators must collaborate to cultivate an environment where students feel motivated to make better choices as a result rather than fearing penalties that come with missteps. Remember, we're not here to create tension-filled environments where every paper airplane launch triggers a mini lockdown!

In conclusion, evaluating discipline policies is an essential process that magnifies opportunities for improvement and allows us to bolster our genuine commitment to student growth. By gathering meaningful data, engaging students, providing educator support, and fostering a thriving school culture, we can refine our discipline approaches and ultimately strive for a happy balance where learning flourishes amidst the wacky antics of youthful exuberance. So, let's roll up our sleeves, dive into the evaluation process, and emerge triumphant - together! Because when it comes to shaping the future of our students, laughter, learning, and a little good-natured chaos can pave the way for success!

PART FIFTEEN
MOTIVATING THE UNMOTIVATED

IDENTIFYING THE ROOT CAUSES OF DISENGAGEMENT

Identifying the root causes of disengagement in students is a bit like trying to locate the last piece of a jigsaw puzzle in a messy classroom. As a retired cop turned special education teacher, I've walked the thin blue line separating the "good" from the "evil". Now I am walking the thin blue line between "motivated" and "unmotivated" and let me tell you, it requires a hefty amount of detective skills. Often, disengagement comes dressed in the incognito outfit of teenage apathy, disguised as slumped shoulders, half-hearted yawns, and the ever-dreaded "I forgot we have a test" routine. So, how do we expose the hidden culprits behind that unmotivated yawning facade? It starts with a powerful magnifying glass.

First, let's get real. High school can feel like the world's longest escape room, where the ultimate prize is to make it to graduation withhout losing your mind - or at least that's the plan. A disengaged student might be battling internal demons, such as anxiety, depression, or what I like to refer to as "my dog ate my motivation." One minute they're staring blankly into space as if they're in a trance, and the next minute, they're pretending to understand the Pythagorean Theorem while the only thing doing the math is their emotional turmoil. This is where I, a veteran of the "you'd better pay attention, or I'll call your mother," approach, try to wave my proverbial police baton and break through the mental fog. It seems like a solid intervention strategy until it only earns me a few disdainful eye rolls and steady glares like I'm trying to cramp their style.

Secondly, let's consider the classroom itself - a fortress of educational insanity. With fluorescent lights buzzing overhead and a lack of cozy corners for daydreaming, students often look for refuge from this chaos. If a classroom feels more like a prison than a place for intellectual flourishing, can we really blame them? I find that creating an inviting space can often persuade students to put their guard down and engage. Consider plants, colorful posters, or even motivational quotes framed like they're valuable works of art. A comfy chair won't hurt either, although I must admit, chairs have a charm of their own. Watching a kid sink into an oversized bean bag chair to calm their mind so that they don't throw a chair through a window, is probably a battle you don't want to fight.

In addition to environmental factors, the curriculum plays a crucial role in guiding students toward - dare I say it - enthusiasm. Nothing kills the spirit quite like writing a five page essay or studying for a test that seems to exist just to torture them. A curriculum that lacks relevance to their reality creates disengagement faster than you can shout "Pop quiz!" We need to integrate real-world applications and find ways to tailor lessons to pique their interest. Yes, I know it sounds like we should be making high school more like a Netflix binge-watching session where students likely engage with "stranger things" instead of actual learning. But seriously, who doesn't enjoy a class where we can mix history with drama or math with baking, because let's face it, who doesn't want to become a master at pizza proportions?

There's also the vital human connection in this crossfire of disengagement. A distressed student is unlikely to open up about their struggles without building trust first. Honestly, it's a one-sided relationship at first. The smallest act of kindness, like a genuine "how's it going?" combined with a dash of humor about my own blunders, can shift the atmosphere. Slowly but surely, I find that laughter becomes the universal language, and humor often paves the road to engagement.

At the end of the day, understanding why students disengage is crucial if we are to address it effectively. It's about getting to the roots of the problem, because once you realize the sticky situations that lead to disengagement, you can help students navigate away from them. Detecting these hidden causes requires persistence and an understanding eye. So, sharpen those detective skills, put on your Sherlock Holmes detective hat, and prepare for the most rewarding wild goose chase of your teaching career! By doing so, we help students not just escape disengagement but discover the joy of learning with a few laughs along the way. And if all else fails, we can always resort to the humane and educational method of bribery - uh, I mean, positive reinforcement, whose ultimate goal is reviving that much-needed spark in our students!

CREATING A COMFORTABLE LEARNING ENVIRONMENT

Creating a comfortable learning environment is a quest and has its positives and negatives. In law enforcement I had the job of creating an interview room and an interrogation room. Well, if you don't know the difference let me explain. While both rooms are used for speaking with people, they are very different in their appearance. The interview room is for speaking with children, victims, witnesses, and anyone else who wants to share information. This room has padded chairs, colorful pictures, crayons and coloring books, and any other item to make people comfortable. The interrogation room has nothing on the walls, no flowers or coloring books, in fact it has a non-padded chair, one desk, and the walls are one color. This room is designed to make people uncomfortable. This is the room where we read Miranda Rights and suspects are asked questions about crimes that we know they committed. It is often used to get a confession. Now that you know the difference, do you want your classroom to look like an interview room, or an interrogation room?

I've seen classrooms that could intimidate even the bravest of adventurers, filled with fluorescent lights and desks lined up like a battalion of overachieving soldiers. So, how does one transform this chaos into something inviting?

First, let's talk about couches and bean bags in the room. When students stride into my classroom, I want them to feel more at ease than they would if they were binge-watching their favorite series on the couch. Gone are the days when sitting up straight was mandatory; we need to embrace the idea that comfort promotes learning. So, I invested in a seriously squishy bean bag, which I swear must have mystical powers because once students plop down, their shoulders immediately drop, and it's like a sigh of relief echoes through the room. It's a steep price to pay, but there's nothing quite like seeing a kid use a bean bag as a makeshift throne, completely ready to engage in whatever activity he's working on.

Next up is the décor. Now, I'm no interior designer, but I firmly believe that a harmonious and inviting environment can significantly influence student motivation. The walls of my team's classroom is adorned with posters featuring quotes about learning that are just as inspirational as they are awkward. A bright color scheme? Check! Plants? Absolutely! So, imagine the curiosity students feel when they walk into a classroom that feels less like a corporate boardroom and more like a gathering of lifelong learners.

Another critical facet of creating a comfortable learning environment is the emotional climate. Trust me; a student can sense a hostile atmosphere faster than a seasoned detective on a stakeout notices suspicious behavior. It's all about building relationships. I strive to be the kind of teacher who students feel comfortable engaging with - someone who knows the delicate balance of a to-the-point "Hey, put that phone down" and a friendly "How's it going?" Some days I've found that beginning class with a corny joke or two sets such a tone that they momentarily forget they're in a classroom and might actually begin to enjoy themselves. Sure, laughter doesn't solve all problems, but catching a student trying to suppress laughter over a chemistry pun might just be the spark we need to ignite learning.

Moreover, let's not forget the power of collaboration. Students thrive in an environment where they can learn from each other, and it quickly dispels the notion that learning is a solitary struggle. Picture this: students working together like a well-oiled pop band instead of playing solo on their instruments. Group work can feel like a recipe for chaos, but when done right, it's like transforming a grumpy cat meme into a viral dance challenge - enjoyable and infectious! I tend to arrange my desks in small clusters that promote interaction, which usually leads to a cacophony of discussions. One minute we're discussing Shakespeare, and the next, a student has established an entirely new theory on why Romeo never texted Juliet back.

In addition to encouragement and comfort, I also put significant effort into embracing differences among students. Creating a comfortable environment means cultivating a space that recognizes everyone's unique backgrounds and learning styles. Employing flexible seating arrangements for those who thrive in different environments or offering up choices for assignments fosters empowerment. I love to think of my classroom as a buffet where everyone can choose their dish - if they want a spicy project or something sweetly simple, all while still aiming toward a common goal.

To sum it up, creating a comfortable learning environment is one tactic of engagement and connection. It's about turning an intimidating classroom full of desks into a welcoming space that helps students feel at home, whether that means diving into academic conversations, sharing laughs, or negotiating ownership of the last bag of chips. It's about interactions and building a sense of community where students can both thrive and feel comfortable taking risks. So, fellow educators, let's gear up, grab our bean bags, because we must raise a generation of comfortable learners ready to conquer their academic challenges one pun at a time!

INCORPORATING HANDS-ON LEARNING EXPERIENCES

Incorporating hands-on learning experiences in the classroom can feel like hosting a wild party where the invitees are reluctant teenagers armed with Snapchat filters and borderline apathy. When I was in law enforcement one of my jobs was being a field training coordinator. I wrote new curricula for all of our new officers. This FTO program involved reading policy, learning how to conduct traffic stops, how we conducted felony stops, and 95% of the program was hands on learning. There are not many professions where you don't have hands on training. Imagine if in law enforcement we never conducted a traffic stop in the FTO program. Now when that officer is on his own, do you think he would be able to stop a vehicle without help? NO! The same goes for education. If I never showed my students how to use jumper cables on a vehicle and let them practice, do you think they could do it for real when their battery dies? NO! The good news is that tangible, engaging activities can turn students from reluctant participants into enthusiastic learners quicker than you can say "Stop Resisting!" So, let's talk about how to weave hands-on learning into our lessons and coax those teenagers into participating with a little less eye-rolling and a bit more excitement.

First off, let me say that most lessons can include a hands-on activity. One of my favorite methods involves turning classic subjects into engaging lessons. For example, numbers and formulas can become a culinary adventure with a little math and a few cooking supplies. It's amazing how quick they are to embrace fractions when they realize a cookie recipe calls for math to be completed. When those fractions determine more cookies for everyone-suddenly the fire of passion ignites, and all of a sudden, we have a lively cookie connoisseurship session unfolding right before us!

Science, too, can be spruced up with some hands-on experimentation. I remember conducting a weather-related science project, complete with DIY weather stations, being met with loud enthusiasm as students dived headfirst into the making of storm clouds using empty soda bottles. It may have looked like chaos - the floor was strewn with cotton balls, and I half-wondered if a weather pattern might spontaneously occur amongst the debris - but the sheer enjoyment on their faces was priceless. There's something downright magical when students grasp concepts through their senses. It's like adding bacon to everything - it makes it irresistible!

They come to understand the atmospheric pressure and humidity in a way that textbooks could never convey, all while having a blast with real life phenomena.

Incorporating hands-on experiences often means embracing

the possibility of some good old-fashioned messiness. I'm not saying we should let them go nuts with glitter (although can you imagine the aftermath?), but minor chaos often comes hand-in-hand with true discovery. I've learned to prepare for a little mayhem-whether it's from paint splatters or the latest "oops, I dropped that!" moment - as it often leads to enlightening conversations. Students learn from their mistakes; suddenly spilled glue becomes a lesson in empathy. "Sorry! it's all over your shoes." We giggle and gather together, using this hiccup as an opportunity for character-building - because hey, nothing says "community" like bonding over shared cleanup!

Another Hail Mary play of hands-on learning is technology integration. By letting students immerse themselves in technology that they're already familiar with, we engage their curiosity in a whole new way. Enter apps and platforms that transform old-school subjects into interactive quests, such as virtual reality journeys matching pictures of ancient civilizations to their historical contexts. It's about connecting the dots, making lessons resonate outside the walls of the classroom. Students love the opportunity to participate and explore, leaving behind the notion of learning as a tedious grind-it suddenly becomes a thrilling mission that might even come with their own subtitles!

So, in conclusion, incorporating hands-on learning experiences isn't just about breaking up the monotony of lectures and worksheets; it's about igniting that elusive connection and curiosity within students. It's about grabbing their attention, much like a cat with a laser pointer - once they see that dot zooming around, they'll put in the effort to chase it down! In our relentless pursuit of engagement, let's ignite these young minds into a realm of tactile exploration, amidst laughter and learning, all while creating memories that they might just carry with them into brighter futures. In the end, education should feel less like a detention hall and more like the wildest science fair on the planet.

ESTABLISHING CLEAR AND ACHIEVABLE GOALS

Establishing clear and achievable goals in the classroom can feel a bit like trying to corral a group of squirrels. Everybody has their own agenda and is often more worried about what they are going to eat for lunch than following your carefully laid-out plan. Just like when I was an officer, I've learned that creating a roadmap of objectives is essential to any great laid out plan like serving a search warrant. Without out a game plan, serving the search warrant could end in a worst case scenario like death. Now just because a poorly laid out plan in the classroom goes south, it doesn't mean worst case scenario like it does in police work. At worst, in the classroom, we may have a bladder explode because someone doesn't make it to the bathroom in time. We know how kids are. They wait till you leave for that four hour trip to say they have to go to the bathroom. But in education, we must steer our delightful band of misfit learners toward success. The trick is to distill these larger-than-life aspirations into easily digestible nuggets that don't send them running for the nearest exit. So, grab a snack-preferably something not too crumbly-and let's dive into how to craft goals that stick!

First, let's talk about clarity. Imagine standing in the middle of a corn maze, desperately searching for the exit while your friends run confidently toward a giant inflatable turkey. That's how students often feel when we toss vague objectives their way. Instead, we need to set them up with clear and concise goals that outline what they are striving for, ensuring no one gets left behind lost in a metaphorical cornfield. When students have a precise understanding of what's expected, there's a higher likelihood they'll engage. I mean, who wants to face that awkward moment of raising their hand to ask "Wait, what are we even supposed to be doing?" It's like asking for directions to a place that has zero signage-just a recipe for confusion and embarrassment!

Next up is the 'achievable' part of our riveting goal-setting saga. Setting an ambitious goal is admirable, but if it feels more like a sprint to the moon than an actual project, we may face some serious pushback. So, we need to cook up goals that are challenging yet realistic enough to be appetizing. A student is less likely to feel motivated if faced with a task that seems so overwhelming it requires a team of superheroes to tackle. I often emphasize smaller milestones like "complete one chapter" instead of "finish the entire book," which feels less like giving them a brick wall to climb and more like providing a fun little steppingstone. In police work I handled all my officer's evaluations. Many times, there was more than one thing they needed to work on and if I threw it all at them at once, it would be counterproductive.

For example, if I have an officer who continuously makes

multiple mistakes on a traffic citation, I would sit down with them and go over one thing at a time. If I said, "your citation writing sucks and you make a lot of mistakes", this doesn't help the officer learn how to correct the issue. By doing this, it leads to the same mistake being made over and over again. In my class it's no different. If we are working on handwriting because the student completes assignments that looks like he wrote it while riding a horse at his ranch over the weekend, I have to move step by step. This is often also in his IEP. But we have to move one step at a time, so we give that student the individualized education that they deserve.

Once we've established clarity and achievability, it's time to write it down and infuse a bit of flair! You see, there's something magical about writing goals that makes them feel more tangible. Together with my students, we identify and jot clown these objectives on colorful sticky notes, plastering them around the classroom like a dazzling arts-and-crafts war room. Who wouldn't feel pumped when they walk into a space filled with bright reminders of their aspirations? Plus, this gives me the chance to add a sprinkle of humor. For instance, "Learn fractions" can be adorned with a doodle of a pizza slice! Because let's be honest, any goal sounds more appetizing when you envision a delicious slice of pizza. I've used the pizza example a lot in this book. Think about it though. When making pizza you have to build that foundation of the perfectly kneaded dough. Once we have that foundation, we can move to the first ingredient, the sauce. Next, we add the cheese followed by the toppings. Education is the same concept. Regardless of the subject, we have to build that strong foundation first. Then let's build on that making topping decisions along the way. Before you know it, you have the best pizza coming out of the oven.

I also encourage my students to find their own personal reasons for each goal. Yea they all have their individual education plan, but student input is so important. The student may have a reading goal in his IEP, but that's an academic goal. What's wrong with setting some personal goals. They don't go into the IEP, but we can write them down in a journal or some other document. It's an essential step that plants the seeds for intrinsic motivation. The classic "I'm just doing this for a good grade" mentality is akin to telling a cat to take a bath. By shifting the focus to their personal growth, it transforms their mindset from obligation to opportunity. Maybe they want to impress their friends, get an ice cream party after acing a project, or - even more outrageous - evoke the pride of their parents. Whatever the motivator may be, when students see how reaching their goals affects their lives, it fosters a sense of ownership that transforms the entire journey!

Continuous feedback is another secret weapon in our quest. Nobody dances well without a little rhythm, right? As students' progress toward their goals, I believe it's crucial to provide feedback to help them stay on track. Testifying in court on a case you lead from beginning to end can be very intimidating. I have had to take the stand in a lot of homicide cases. After your testimony, which could take days, I reflect on how I did. I know there are always things I could improve on, so I would reach out to the District Attorney for feedback. In order to get better at your job, you have to have feedback. It's no different than giving feedback to your students.

Regular check-ins bring a bit of accountability; however, I like to ensure that feedback feels more like a high-five than a scolding. "Hey! You are super close! Just a quick left turn and you'll hit the target!" I've discovered that offering encouragement, even in the face of minor setbacks, creates a thriving learning environment where students feel safe to stumble without fearing the final exam hovercraft descending upon them.

Finally, let's not forget the beauty of celebrating achievements, no matter how small! Picture this: a classroom full of young scholars, each one waltzing over their goals. Recognizing and celebrating even the tiniest steps toward their larger goals fosters positivity. Chocolate cupcakes? Yes, please! A hall of fame featuring students' goal achievements? Absolutely! Celebrations inject excitement into the mundane, allowing students to recognize their potential and believe that their dreams can indeed be achieved, one quirky little step at a time.

To wrap it all up, establishing clear and achievable goals isn't just a checklist exercise. It's about transforming a potentially daunting task into an engaging adventure that allows students to thrive. By providing clarity, ensuring achievability, personalizing the experience, delivering positive feedback, and honoring milestones, we empower our students to chase their aspirations. After all, a well-defined goal is more than a target; it's a rocket fuel that can launch our students into their own success stories - hopefully complete with a few laughs and a heaping dose of joy along the way. So, let's roll up our sleeves, mark our calendars with a bright red "GO!" and embark on this fantastic journey together!

BUILDING A SUPPORTIVE COMMUNITY

Building a supportive community in the classroom feels like attempting to construct a fortress out of marshmallows - not the most sturdy of projects, but somehow, when it all comes together, it's surprisingly delightful! As a retired cop-turned-special education teacher, I can confidently say that fostering a sense of community among students is one of the most crucial elements in creating an enriching learning environment. Think about it: when students feel supported, they not only learn better, but they no longer question whether they should use their "study" breaks to sneak apps on their phones during painful lectures. So, let's roll up our sleeves and discover how to craft a cozy, supportive classroom community that encourages growth and hilarity!

First, let's tackle the human connection that fuels community. Establishing relationships built on trust and respect is essential, and believe me, it's not just a matter of donning a silly hat and cracking jokes. Sure, a few well-timed dad jokes can break the ice, but beneath the comedic facade lies genuine care. I make it a point to get to know each student personally - what makes chem tick, what foods they despise (spoiler: Brussels sprouts), and even what makes them laugh. I've learned that small things like sharing a corny joke or reminiscing over an awkward childhood story help foster a safe space where they can express themselves without fear of judgment. One minute, we're discussing a challenging math problem, and the next, we're all in stitches over a student's uncanny impression of a sea lion chat somehow also relates to their homework. It's all about finding common ground where laughter creates unbreakable bonds!

Next, it's essential to encourage communication and active participation in the classroom. In a supportive community, the students shouldn't feel like they're trapped inside a glass box waiting for someone to break the silence. I've transformed our routines to emphasize group discussions, brainstorming sessions, and even some lively debates. By creating opportunities for students to share their thoughts and opinions, I watch them blossom into confident communicators, as thrilling as watching a plant grow towards the sunlight - if, of course, that plant were actually discussing the finer points of algebra with a sprinkle of sass. I encourage them to express disagreement respectfully, showing them that contrasting views can lead to knowledge and understanding. What better way to bond than having a friendly argument over the merits of pineapple on pizza or the legacy of Shakespeare's most tragic heroes?

Group activities can be the cherry on top of this supportive community sundae. Instead of creating an environment obsessed with competition, I emphasize collaboration. When students work together on projects, magic happens! Picture a room full of students huddled together as they build contraptions for a science fair, their laughter echoing amidst occasional "Oops! We just launched the marshmallow cannon straight into the ceiling!" moments. These tasks create opportunities for teamwork and build trust as they learn to lean on each other's strengths and support one another's weaknesses. This collaboration not only helps them succeed academically but also fosters friendships that extend beyond classroom walls. Suddenly, acquaintances become confidants, and students are empowered to navigate the high school maze together rather than stumbling around alone!

Alongside collaboration, let us sprinkle in the importance of embracing uniqueness - because every student is as distinct as a snowflake and, yes, just as beautifully complex. I strive to cultivate an inclusive environment where each student feels accepted and appreciated. Consider it my mission to create a potluck of personalities - where differences are celebrated like the confetti at a parade - allowing each individual to contribute their unique flavor to the community. Whether through cultural appreciation events or talent showcases, I encourage students to share their backgrounds and interests with their peers. Letting a budding artist showcase their work reinforces the idea that self-expression enriches our learning environment. It reminds students that they're part of a vibrant tapestry rather than just monotonous threads blending into a dull landscape.

In addition, providing social-emotional support is key to nurturing a healthy community. Sometimes, life can throw curveballs more unexpected than my attempts at baking! I tirelessly emphasize the importance of mental well-being, which fosters a supportive environment. Whether that involves hosting "Wellness Wednesdays" featuring yoga, meditation, or even guided discussions on emotional intelligence, initiating these conversations allows students to share feelings, express concerns, and learn coping strategies.

The magic happens when they realize they aren't alone - everyone has their quirky moments where they just need a little support. Suddenly, a safe haven emerges, turning stress into shared smiles and laughter, no more than a subtle invitation to put the "fun" in "fundamental emotional awareness." To sum it up, building a supportive community is vital for student growth both academically and personally. It requires human connections rooted in trust, communication that encourages openness, collaboration that fosters teamwork, acceptance of individuality, and a commitment to mental well-being. By focusing on the bonds formed and aligning our efforts with laughter and understanding, we create an atmosphere where students thrive and feel valued. In our whimsical castle made of marshmallows, every joy and success can be celebrated, and every tear can be met with compassion. So, let's embrace the idea that unity, support, and flexibility come together like the perfect ingredients for an exciting journey in learning. Together, we'll create a tapestry of joy, resilience, and unforgettable memories-complete with a few laughs along the way!

PART SIXTEEN
THE IMPORTANCE OF PROFESSIONAL DEVELOPMENT

THE IMPORTANCE OF LIFELONG LEARNING

When I first became a police officer, my department didn't have a training budget. Every single training I went to was paid for out of my pocket. I was constantly looking for training that I knew would make me better at my job. I would travel across the state on my own dime for accident reconstruction training. I would travel to other states to attend drug interdiction training or Hostage Negotiation training. In my mind these were trainings that I found to be essential to my career. I use this information to explain how important learning is in the classroom. I often tell my students that the learning never stops, even when the school bell rings. I'm not talking about the kind of learning that ends with a final exam and a nice little diploma - but the lifelong learning kind. You know, the "let's discover what makes the world tick" sort of learning that carries on well past the classroom door. Lifelong learning is my personal motto, and I'm here to impart that wisdom to you, whether you like it or not!

Now, once again, let me take you back to my days as a police officer. There I was, donning my uniform, handcuffs jingling, and a hefty dose of self-importance, thinking I had seen it all. But even in the midst of mayhem, I realized something profound: the world doesn't stand still. Just like my waistline after a few too many donuts during the late-night shift, knowledge expands, shifts, and grows. And if I wanted to keep handling situations like a pro-and, let's face it, maybe dodge a citizen's arrest by some overly enthusiastic teenager, I needed to keep learning.

Fast forward a few years, and I traded the badge for a teacher's nameplate. Who knew I'd be swapping the thrill of a high-speed chase for "Okay class, let's find out who forgot to turn in their homework?" I quickly discovered that the teaching profession is not a monolith; it's ever evolving. Just as police methods change with the introduction of new technology and trends, education adapts too. If I wanted to be effective, I had to stay informed and relevant. Hence, lifelong learning became not just a suggestion, but a necessity.

Let's face it, certified teachers are probably the only people who need to attend as many professional development workshops as they do hot dinners. The good news? Many of these workshops are wildly beneficial. Sure, some can feel like watching paint dry while listening to a PowerPoint presentation trying to explain the benefits of dandelion tea (trust me, it's weird), but when the right training session comes along, BAM! Knowledge hits you like a ton of bricks. You walk away like a superhero, equipped with strategies to engage your students better. You become the "Bat-teacher," swooping in to save the day, armed with new tactics.

Let's not forget about the magic of networking! Lifelong

learning isn't just about what happens inside the classroom; it's about building bridges. Every conversation with fellow educators feels like throwing a fishing line into the great big sea of knowledge. Who knows what you might reel in? Suddenly, you're swapping tips on handling the latest rowdy classroom trends, or sharing how you survived the treacherous waters of teacher-parent conferences-those scenarios that carry as much tension as that first courtroom testimony.

But here's where I'll hit you with some salty wisdom - growth doesn't happen in a vacuum. You owe it to yourself to reflect on your journey. After every workshop, ask yourself what you've learned and how you can apply it.

I have always said that you can go to as many trainings as you want, but if you can't apply what you've learned, then that training meant nothing. You have to apply it and reflect on how to apply it. You might be thinking, "Ugh, reflecting sounds like homework, Josh." I hear you but think of it as introspection without the pressure of knowing a pop quiz is lurking around the corner. Pretend you're sitting at the "weight room for the mind," pumping away at those brain muscles, making sure they stay fit and focused.

Let me also add that embracing lifelong learning isn't just about personal benefit. It sends a message to your students too. It's like saying, "Hey, not only am I working on me, but hey, learning is a lifelong gym membership for your brain - no fees, just gains!" When they watch us learning and growing, it plants the seed in their minds that education doesn't stop at graduation - nor does it end when a kid's favorite band drops an album. It's an invitation to them to join the learning adventure.

In essence, lifelong learning keeps our minds sharp, our strategies fresh, and our occasional nightmares about students losing their shoes - less terrifying. So, embrace it! Join a new workshop. Talk to someone you'd usually steer clear of in the teachers' lounge. Trust me, it pays off, because, after all, the journey is not just about teaching the youth; it's about continually evolving into the best version of yourself.

SETTING PROFESSIONAL DEVELOPMENT GOALS

Setting professional development goals might feel like standing in front of a buffet - overwhelming, with all those options just begging for your attention. Maybe you want to hone your skills in classroom management, or perhaps you'd like to dive deep into the art of empathy without turning into an emotional sponge. The possibilities are immense, yet it's all too easy to load your plate with everything you see, leading to an unmanageable heap of tasks that you inevitably abandon while wondering why you're left with a bad case of "I only half-finished all five workshops" syndrome. As a retired cop, I can't stress enough how critical it is to navigate this buffet wisely.

To begin with, you've got to earmark specific, measurable goals - yes, I know; "SMART" goals, that fine acronym that gets thrown around in endless workshops like confetti at a high school pep rally. Specific means pinpointing what you want to achieve. Instead of saying, "I want to improve my teaching," try "I want to implement three new interactive techniques to drive engagement." This clarity takes you from simply nibbling on the hors d'oeuvres to going straight for the main course. Just like how I wouldn't march into a departments kitchen and claim I can cook, merely because I've made a PB&J-no, I have to really plan my culinary ambitions!

Next comes (M) the measurable part, which is crucial. This isn't like trying to measure your dog's love by counting how many times he brings you his chew toy - though that might work in a pinch! Rather, think about how you will measure your success. If you want to try out those three new techniques, establish how you'll check your progress. Maybe it involves gathering student feedback, monitoring their energy levels, and/or checking if their homework magically appears from under the couch for once! Don't just wing it; set clear indicators so you know when you're hitting the bullseye (like, "Yes, they're actually paying attention," or "no, they didn't just fall asleep with their heads on their desks").

Now, let's discuss the pesky "A" attainable. I'm all for aiming high; just don't aim for the stars while forgetting that you need a working rocket ship first. Goals should challenge you but also be rooted in the reality of your situation. Picture it: you can't strategize to lead the next education reform while knee-deep in grading papers and trying to offer emotional support to that one student who insists on doing their math homework in crayon. Strive for balance-make sure your goals align with what's practical amidst the chaos often found in any school setting.

Remember, you've got to put a timeline on it-a deadline that keeps your feet to the fire but doesn't send you screaming for the hills. I know that you're already juggling an endless list of responsibilities, but having a timeline helps you prioritize. It's like my gym regime; I don't just say, "I will lift weights someday." No, I put Monday, Tuesday, Wednesday, Thursday, Friday, and Saturday in my calendar as "Lift Days," and nothing else matters - unless I'm trying to dodge a donut run with my police buddies. Set those deadlines for your professional development goals with purpose, whether it's quarterly reviews or semester check-ins - whatever keeps you accountable without overwhelming you.

Here we are at the (R) results-oriented. Don't forget to sprinkle in a pinch of flexibility. Life in a school is like a game of Jenga, and just as you think you're getting it all under control, something happens. Perhaps a student decides today is the day they want to impersonate a goat, or the Wi-Fi goes down. But when we set our goals, we to make sure that what goals we put in place are easy to evaluate. We need to remember that our goals must be evaluated on whether or not the results are what we expected. Are we evaluating our progress fairly and honestly. We can evaluate both directly and indirectly. I'm not saying that we have to see if we made progress on a goal at the end of every week. We also don't need all numbers and stats to evaluate progress. Sometimes the success of reaching your goals can shine through at the least expected times. Remember, reaching those goals doesn't mean that success slaps you in the face. Often when we reflect, we realize that we did make progress on that goal.

As you tackle your professional development landscape, we want to make sure your goals have some sort of time frame (T). Set goals that are both short term and long term. An example of a short-term goal could be making sure you catch up on grading every two weeks. Maybe another short-term goal addresses management in your class. Long term goals could be taking a specific training or implementing more technology in your lessons.

Lastly, even though it is not part of the SMART acronym, reflecting may be one of the most important things. After each completed goal, just like after an exquisite meal, take a moment to savor what you've accomplished. Celebrate your small wins! Be it through a high-five with a colleague or yelling "I did it!" in front of your class. Recognizing progress keeps you motivated and reminds you that you're not just working to improve your teaching but continuously evolving and becoming a better version of yourself. It's the most important way to advance your career as you dish up the best for your students. So, get out there, set those professional development goals, and feast on knowledge like a pro!

PART SEVENTEEN
CELEBRATING ACHIEVEMENTS

THE IMPORTANCE OF RECOGNITION IN STUDENT DEVELOPMENT

Let me tell you a little secret about human nature: we all love recognition. Whether it's a thumbs-up emoji on social media or having your favorite teacher slap a shiny gold star on your paper, who doesn't want a little validation now and then? When I transitioned from wearing a badge to wielding a whiteboard marker, I realized that the same is true for my students. Recognition in education isn't just some feel-good fluff; it's a fundamental part of student development. Trust me, I've seen it all, from brawny kids who can bench press a bus to artistic souls who can barely lift their heads from a sketchbook; all of them can flourish when we recognize their achievements.

First off, let's talk about the peculiar time warp that is high school. It's a strange place where hormones run wild, and kids oscillate between feeling invincible one minute and completely invisible the next. In this chaotic time, recognition acts like a lighthouse in foggy waters, guiding our young sailors to safety. I mean, how many times have I seen a kid's face light up after hearing, "Great job on your project!"? Once, I looked up from my desk during an exam to see one student literally face-first in the papers, likely believing that if he missed another question, he'd miss out on the secret to life. But when he was called out for his effort, he transformed from "The Human Paperweight" into "The Light of Recognition!" It's like I had just installed a mood ring for classroom morale.

Now, recognition doesn't just elevate morale; it genuinely fosters a growth mindset. When we acknowledge a student for a small victory - whether they finally nailed that algebra problem or turned in an essay without a single grammar mistake-they start to believe that their hard work can lead to success. Suddenly, they're motivated to tackle the next challenge instead of hiding behind their backpacks. As a retired cop turned educator, I can appreciate the importance of encouraging kids to confront challenges head-on; after all, if I could chase down a horse thief in my day, my students can certainly face those geometry angles with some encouragement!

Let's be real, recognition isn't just about pats on the back or shiny stickers. The key is making it meaningful. I recall a student defrosting into enthusiasm like a popsicle in the sun when she received a student of the month award from me praising her effort in class. The glowing review wasn't just some random selection from a greeting card shop; it was a sincere acknowledgment of her hard work that made her want to keep striving.

Recognition can be diverse, too; it's not only about academic achievements. Let's not forget the basketball star who chose to grab a Gatorade over his textbook (hey, hydration is important, too). Recognizing team players instills a sense of belonging in students, helping them to realize that they're part of something larger than themselves. On that basketball court, when he finally got some playing time, I was the first one he told.

It didn't matter if he played for 1 minute or 5 minutes, it was important enough for him to tell me and I congratulated him. I reality, I may have been the only one to recognize his accomplishment.

But beware, let's avoid the slippery slope of over-recognition! We don't want it to become a game of "Who Can Collect the Most Ribbons?" In my police days, I learned that too much acknowledgment could lead to nonsense, just like too much sugar leads to a classroom full of hyperactive gremlins. Moderation is key. Find that balance, and make recognition fun, light-hearted, and downright memorable.

In the end, recognition in the classroom paves the way for lifelong learners who embrace their unique paths. It's not about stuffing students into cookie-cutter molds; it's about creating an environment where accomplishments - big and small - are acknowledged and celebrated, laying down the groundwork for resilience and success. My ambition? To watch every student revel in their moment of glory while balancing it with humor, warmth, and a solid gold star on their path to success.

PART EIGHTEEN
LOOKING AHEAD: PREPARING FOR GRADUATION

UNDERSTANDING POST-HIGH SCHOOL OPTIONS

I currently have some seniors that I am working with who will be entering the real world. This can be intimidating especially when they still don't have an idea of what they want to do. A lot of those seniors are athletes and having been an athlete myself in high school, I sometimes share advice about post high school goals. I have a quote hanging up in my office as well as my weight room at home. It says, "The barbell teaches you a different lesson. The barbell holds the opportunities of getting stronger, ability to change your body, and build resolve. BUT (and this is the important part) the barbell doesn't give a shit about you.

You pick it up and it gives you positive, life-changing results, or you don't, and gives you NOTHING. The barbell doesn't care one way or another. It looks you right in the face and says, "This is going to be hard, and it is going to take a lot of work, but the pay-off is going to be awesome. Take it or leave it" in today's society, it's a lesson many need to learn. Life is a barbell! The opportunities are right there. You simply need to pick them up and start GRINDING.

It's all on you. It has always been. It will always be." Sometimes this advice can really hit home for those who work out. The meaning makes sense when they decide to keep pushing a trust the process.

My journey into the chaotic world of high school was a bit like trying to navigate through a room full of teenagers who had just discovered the concept of hormones. And trust me, if you think your average high school hall is confusing, just wait until graduation season rolls around! Suddenly, it seems like students become stuck in a whirlwind of options, each one spinning faster than the last, filled with all sorts of plans, dreams, and more stress than a police officer during a donut shortage.

Let's set the scene a little clearer: understanding your post-high school options is like figuring out the ending to a mystery novel where every character is on a different pathway bursting with possibilities, and you're left to decide what's best for you.

First and foremost, you've got the beloved higher education route. Ah, yes, college - with its promises of freedom, adventure, and the occasional existential crisis. It's where kids go to declare their majors, only to switch them a dozen times while learning how to survive on Ramen noodles. Parents beam with pride as their kids officially enroll in school. For some, it's an exploration of knowledge that can lead to a bright and shiny career. For others, well, let's just say that if you can major in procrastination with a minor in Memes, some students would offer you a thesis. I often joke that if we could turn studeents' late-night social media scrolling into a college credit, we'd have a nation of scholars!

Let's talk about the vocational route - also known as the practical approach to adulthood. Here, students can explore apprenticeships, trade schools, and certifications that can catapult them into the workforce faster than you can say "I'll take a double espresso, please." Imagine a world where high school seniors can actually become plumbers or electricians with skills that just might pay off their student loans before they even think about getting them. They might be the very ones laughing all the way to the bank while their buddies are stuck working part-time at a coffee shop trying to afford their fourth semester of Philosophy, which, let's be honest, has done little more than teach them how to chat about their feelings while consuming overpriced lattes.

Let's not forget our merry friends at the job market: while some students want to climb the corporate ladder, others are more interested in figuring out just how far they can get without ever putting shoes on - those essential "work-from-home" shoes that equate to socks and slippers. For some, straight into the workforce is the noble answer. But let's face it; telling your parents you want to skip college to become a professional "only fans" dancer might not go over well at the Sunday dinner table. It may require some creative explanations - after all, who wouldn't want to leave school and instantly enter a world where your biggest responsibility is deciding which viral dance challenge to tackle next? As students weigh these options, they often seem blissfully unaware of what they're signing up for. They're in it for the adventure.

For students who want to earn a diploma, graduation is like a rite of passage. A rite that their parents accomplished and now its passed on to their own kids.

DEVELOPING LIFE SKILLS FOR INDEPENDENCE

The glorious transition from high school senior to an independent adult- a time when the world opens up like a bear trap, and suddenly students realize that living on their own means more than just getting away with staying up late, eating pizza for breakfast, and having a laundry basket that only gets emptied every other week. Developing life skills for independence is the grand quest that every soon-to-be graduate embarks upon, and if they're not careful, it can result in hilarious misadventures that would make great reality TV. Let's talk about some of these life skills.

I don't know about you, but who else learned how to sew and cook in the home economics class in high school? My school doesn't have this kind of class so instead of complaining about how my students don't go to class to learn how to cook, I bring the cooking to them. In my classes, we not only focus on goals and objectives, but we do a lot of life skills training. One of the things I teach in class is geared towards developing lifelong skills.

For example, we do a career unit where we first created an account on Career Builder. Students then enter information about themselves that help them write resumes and cover letters. We talk about how to choose the proper references and how we go about filling out applications. As we move forward in this career unit, we talk about what to wear to an interview and the different types of dress that's appropriate.

Students learn how to tie a tie and how to use jumper cables in case their vehicle won't start. You can't get to an interview unless you have a ride. In addition to career preparation, we also cook and learn how to follow a recipe. Just before summer break, students get trained in CPR and First Aid. These are just some of the things I do that I hope some day will benefit them on this journey called life. Let's look at some of these things in a little more depth.

First off, let's talk about budgeting. There's a reason why so many students view money management like it's an impending root canal - nobody wants to do it, but they know they have to. Learning to crack expenses, create a budget, and figuring out how much they're pouring into their daily Starbucks habit may just be the most crucial lesson they never learned in math class. They need to remember; every latte is one step closer to living in their parents' basement indefinitely!

Next on that illustrious life skill checklist is cooking. This is an essential skill for survival that far too many graduates over-look in their quest to become masters of the microwave. I learned how to cook in high school and from my mother who didn't want me to disappoint my future wife. Developing some basic cooking skills is not just about avoiding scurvy; it's about retaining some level of dignity when you invite friends over and confidently announce that "yes, I did make this lasagna from scratch... and no, the smoke detector never went off.

Hold on, there's more-perhaps an even bigger challenge awaits them. Shocker, it's the mysterious land of cleaning! No one quite tells students that "cleaning" doesn't mean shoving everything into the closet and hoping for the best. The delicate art of balancing cleanliness with reckless abandon can often lead to them discovering what lay at the bottom of their dorm fridge - a science experiment that has come to life and has the potential to take over the world. Teaching them the basics-vacuuming, laundry techniques, and using a mop, will help transform that cluttered space into a livable dorm room complete with no mammals squatting.

And finally, we have the most underestimated skill of them all-the art of asking for help. For many, this feels like admitting defeat, along the lines of running a marathon while shouting "I'm tired!" to the world. But guess what? Asking for assistance is often the first step toward building a support system that can turn chaos into manageable pieces. Whether it's seeking help from parents, guidance from a mentor, leaning on friends for support, or connecting with local community resources, understanding that no one is expected to navigate life alone is a beautiful revelation that leads to lifelong independence.

A these soon-to-be graduates stumble forward into the wild unknown, let's remind them that developing life skills for independence is not just about checking off items on a checklist. It's a unique blend of chaos, hilarity, and the occasional mishap that ultimately shapes them into adults. Let them realize that their independence is an epic journey; it's about savoring the victories and laughing at the misadventures. Welcome to adulthood - where the food is sometimes burnt, but the lessons are priceless!

CLOSURE

Holy SCHNIKES! That was a lot of writing! Here we are at the end of a long book, and I hope you gained some insight into how being a police officer has played a role in my transition back to teaching. A lot of ideas and strategies I use have come from my years in law enforcement. Being a cop isn't just about handling calls for service and taking people to jail. I often found myself wearing many hats. I was a counselor, a referee, an educator, a parent, (for the ones who didn't know how to parent), a disciplinarian, and a coach. Education is no different. You often can't start your day until you put on the old parent cap and remind your students why breakfast is important. The things I talk about in this book aren't groundbreaking pieces of information. In fact, a lot of it we already know. But it doesn't hurt to review and read things from a different perspective. Whether you are a principal, counselor, teacher, or coach, we are all in this together. We are all on the same team and we sometimes just need a reminder to keep pushing. We definitely are not in education for the money, so let's keep doing it for the students. It's those unique and sometimes annoying humans that need our love and support. Remember, our reward for doing this job comes not from our success, but from the successes of our students.